Diary of a Change Agent

This book is dedicated to consultants, clients and everyone throughout the world who is interested in creating value with, and through, other people.

Diary of a Change Agent

Tony Page

Gower

Published by
Gower Publishing Limited
Gower House
Croft Road
Aldershot
Hampshire GU11 3HR
England

Gower
Old Post Road
Brookfield
Vermont 05036
USA

British Library Cataloguing in Publication Data
Page, Tony
Diary of a change agent
1. Organizational change 2. Reengineering (Management)
3. Organizational behaviour
I. Title
658.4'06

ISBN 0 566 07779 5

Library of Congress Cataloging-in-Publication Data
Page, Tony, 1955-
Diary of a change agent/by Tony Page.
p.   cm.
Includes bibliographical references and index.
ISBN 0-566-07779-5
1. Organizational change. 2. Organizational change—Case studies.
I. Title.
HD58.8.P34   1996   98–13840
658.4'08—dc20   CIP

Typeset in Palatino by Wileman Design and printed in Great Britain
by the University Press, Cambridge.

Contents

Foreword

This is a courageous and timely volume which makes absorbing reading and will challenge every consultant and client who is willing to be in the least introspective about their quest for personal, professional and commercial value. It may be too close for the comfort of those who still believe that consulting is about rational analysis only, but those prepared to pay the price of self-examination will find it a bargain in terms of the personal insights, professional development and commercial opportunities that Tony's method and models open up.

The diary is a brave and refreshingly frank account of Tony's work as a successful Change Management Consultant, during a critical three-year period. His personal revelations underline how much one's *self* is an integral part of the consulting process and how the internal and external worlds of client and consultant must touch and interact in the search for *value*.

A personal diary or professional journal of hypotheses about client-consultant relationships can be a life-enhancing consulting tool. To be able to understand *feelings* as well as *facts* is an essential, active ingredient of a consultant's work.

Tony embraces the spirit of lifelong learning and continuing professional development so this book will be a *vade mecum* for change managers in search of value at every age and stage. It is already on the required reading list for all consultants attending the Maresfield Curnow Management Consulting Skills Programme of which Tony himself is a distinguished alumnus.

Barry Curnow
President of the Institute of
Management Consultants
21 January 1996

Acknowledgements

I would like to thank my clients for supporting and trusting me to work with them as their consultant. It takes two to tango and, without them, my work, this book and creating value would not be possible.

I would like to thank those who read lengthy, tortuous early drafts of the book. They helped me with their constructive comments and pointed me in the direction of greater reader interest and value.

I would like to thank my mother and father who through my upbringing challenged me to reconcile the competing pressures of human versus commercial values.

Declaration and disclaimer

The publication of this book is intended to create value by illuminating for us all, the complex, dynamic human relationship between people at work. It is not intended to harm or embarrass anyone.

The book contains subjective impressions clouded by the writer's mood at the time of writing each entry. It reveals the writer's prejudices, patterns and habits of observation and description rather than the true character, strengths or weaknesses of the individuals involved. This is perception, not real and not 'the truth' in any absolute sense; neither are the writer's perceptions always complete or well rounded.

The truth about other people is in a sense already 'out there' in the public perception of them, reflected time after time in their many daily interactions. Anything written here that is true is, by and large, observable by others. Anything written here that is untrue or misleading can also be judged by others. The harm done in such cases is to the writer's own reputation and credibility rather than to the person observed.

I have attempted to preserve the truth of each situation as I myself perceived it at the time. Names have been changed where appropriate, and the identities of people and companies have been disguised to protect them.

Part 1
INTRODUCTION

Why read this book?

I am Tony Page. I am a management consultant. I am 40. Although this is the start of a book, it feels as if I am beginning at the end, like a round-the-world yachtsman who has just completed a harrowing three-year adventure and like Gulliver returning from his travels, I am eager to convey my insights but risk being misunderstood. This book is my account of the journey, the insights and a demonstration of a learning method.

My 40 years have been an adventure in which I have learned plenty about life, about people, organizations and business. But the last three years were qualitatively different. New and unexpected professional challenges presented themselves. I started to see things differently. I gained a new perspective, putting several pieces of a personal jigsaw into place and gaining a bigger picture. I made up my mind about some of the important and recurring dilemmas at those difficult intersections between personal, professional and corporate life. In the process I learned much about who I am, where I'm going, what I want to be and the kind of work I want to do. I learned about how I can give value to, get value from and create value with other people.

Creating value through other people

I wrote a diary originally for myself, to help me gain perspective on life. Then I realized that what was written could be of interest and value to others and I wrote it up as a book. At first it was 'a book by a consultant for other consultants' but in this final draft I recognize the wider appeal to all managers, directors, chief executives, service providers, clients and leaders of change. So this book is not only for consultants, it is also for many of you who do not call yourselves consultants but have something important in common with consultants – that is, you do your business with and through other people. Your business success depends on creating value through a human interface.

In a sense we are all striving to create value in our lives. We all want something more: perhaps more money, more time, more appreciation, a better job, better relationships, something meaningful, a better life. But we are not isolated. We operate with other people, through relationships. We act as 'agents', offering our skills and expertise, combining our energies with friends, colleagues, clients, employers to create value for others.

Many of our relationships with other people are within the framework of a larger organization. Increasingly our organizations are run by business values such as performance, efficiency, improvement and competitiveness. Intruding from the host organization(s) into every person-to-person relationship is an external pressure to perform, to change, to win. With each new wave of change, the pressures, the stress and the levels of frustration in the relationship build up.

Beyond the pinball mentality

In the final years of this century we are living in the brave new, competitive, turbulent world and being bombarded with unprecedented amounts of information and advice. There is a publishing boom in management books. Personal development, business psychology and self-help are all big business. Gurus such as Tom Peters, Richard Pascale and Anthony Robbins travel the world, impressing huge conferences with solutions that will revolutionize the results gained by corporations and by the people who work in them.

Instead of benefiting from this proliferation of information, we seem to suffer under the weight of it. We lose our direction. We become confused. We confuse our clients. We add to the turbulence. In my own professional field I notice that we seem to bounce around like pinballs from cushion to cushion: *ding* 'Total Quality Management' . . . *dong* 'Activity-based Costing' . . . *ding* '360° Feedback' . . . *dong* 'Business Process Re-engineering' . . . *ding* 'Change Management' . . . *dong* 'The Learning Organization'.

The pinball game is not all bad: the move from fad to fad challenges our complacency and allows us to pick up new ideas, but something more is needed to achieve a real sustainable change or improvement to our results. It is as if we keep missing the point. It is as if the information and advice never really touches us deeply. We think we have got it but we haven't. We separate ourselves from it by a glass wall. We do not know how to take it in. We do not know how to 'walk the talk'. We do not know how to learn.

A blockage to learning and competitive performance

A quotation given by a speaker at a recent conference expressed this learning problem with chilling clarity:

> We are going to win and the industrial West is going to lose; there is not much you can do about it because the reasons for your failure are within yourselves. . . . We are beyond your mind set. Business . . . is now so complex and difficult . . . continued existence depends on the day to day mobilisation of every ounce of intelligence. (Konosuke Matsushita, Founder, Matsushita Electric)

I agree that there is plenty we are getting wrong in business. There is a very slow absorption of new ideas into business practice. Most businesses still operate from a mechanistic, pre-Einstein and pre-Theory Y mind set. The management knowledge of the 1940s and 1950s from Lewin, Deming and McGregor is still not adopted. Yet we are pumping out more and more ideas: Theory Y has been superseded by Theory Z and Beyond Theory Z. There is a denial of the human dimension to business. In many business circles it is still considered 'soft' to recognize that, beyond the shareholder, there are other 'stakeholders' such as employees, suppliers and customers with honourable and probably longer-term interests in the success of a business. There is a fearful and desperate clinging on to old methods that do not work. There are leadership mistakes including exploitation, propaganda, dishonest manipulation, exhortation and hypocrisy. Consequently we can see frustration, pretended commitment, dependency, lack of trust, lip service and layer upon layer of denial and resistance.

Overcoming the Matsushita curse

But I do not subscribe to the idea that Westerners are doomed to failure. Why? I sense a hunger for a reliable, logical means of overcoming the learning block that Matsushita has highlighted. Also, I sense that, after many disappointing change initiatives in business, we are starting to realize where to look for a solution.

> Our individual context is our hidden strategy for dealing with life. It determines all the choices we make. (Goss, Pascale and Athos, *Harvard Business Review*.)

We are finally recognizing what is central to creating change, to learning, to generating value together and therefore to business performance. We are realizing that we need individuals to take responsibility, to see what is real and what is possible, then honestly to pursue value in cooperation with others. A winning organization supports individuals working together to create value for all the stakeholders. A successful business formula today is much more about trust than about control.

Bringing this knowledge into use by the individual is still the challenge. Old habits are deeply ingrained. The glass wall between knowing and doing is still in place. Beyond that is another glass wall between doing and being or believing. For an organization to force or prescribe that individuals must change, learn or 'behave as if' is counterproductive. It is more top-down control. It leads to more denial, more resistance, more dishonesty, more pretended commitment.

A personal re-engineering method

This book is quite simply giving you and other individuals a means to bring any new knowledge into use. It is the antidote to the pinball tendency. It builds a pathway from new ideas to solidity, coherence and strength. It is not an easy journey. In a way it is like a personal method of business process re-engineering, stripping down old worn-out work processes to the core, then rebuilding more efficient, more effective processes. You will be exposing the core values and assumptions that are driving you, then examining and retuning them.

Your journey crosses boundaries between many disconnected worlds. Consider, for example, the following everyday disconnections and contradictions:

- business versus personal life
- facts versus feelings
- subjective versus objective
- your best interests versus others' best interests.

By examining contradictions, discovering tensions, noticing instead of ignoring slight feelings of discomfort and asking yourself questions you are opening up to valuable learning. You can start to develop a proficiency in reconciling opposites, discovering enduring answers to difficult questions, finding your deeply held beliefs and values, trying and evaluating new ways of operating. You can start to see your world with new eyes, hear new sounds, smell new smells. Your heightened awareness fuels the creative work of reintegration, synthesis and personal transformation.

This book gives you an example of a journey of transformation in the form of extracts from three years of my diary. Some readers may choose to take this in passively, gazing across at someone else's life, like watching a TV documentary. I am hoping you will gain something much more than this: an opportunity to reflect and learn. As you read, issues and feelings may rise up inside you. The active learning opportunity is to face squarely and tackle these issues.

The reflective challenge

Many of us enjoy activity. We lead busy lives. We operate under pressure. We fight to win. But our activist tendency inhibits our reflective learning and locks us into a repeating present. This is the Matsushita curse. This book challenges you to prove Matsushita wrong, to wake up and mobilize every ounce of your intelligence. By doing this you can gain specific pay-offs both at the business and at the personal level and you can find new ways to create value at the human interface.

The book shows you a logical method for personal transformation that is also the key to corporate transformation. It is a method for continuous personal learning. It is the personal competitive advantage you need to survive in the turbulent business environment.

Why the book was written

Trapped in an activist pattern

At the beginning of 1993, I felt I was racing through life – like driving in the outside lane of a motorway at 90 mph, the scenery was flashing past. I had very little sense of control and a rather low awareness of what I was leaving behind me.

Five years earlier I had resigned from PA Consulting Group, choosing to have a personal life rather than allowing an exciting career to dominate. Since then I had worked as an independent consultant, coping with the swings of fortune from feast to famine and back again. Initially I had struggled, then in partnership with a market research company I built the business up to four consultants and two assistants. I tried continually to get the interpersonal dynamics right and build an effective team but I kept coming up against my personal tendency to perfectionism, overcontrolling others and a difficulty with trusting. Early in 1992, frustrated at our lack of progress and frightened by the rising overhead costs, I lost faith, gave the others notice and cut right back to me and a part-time secretary. There were a couple of long-term clients but no firm business, and I had no idea of what the future held. I was married with a young family. My wife, Helen, also a management consultant, was dividing her time between working at Shell, her parental role and unpaid work (PTA, school governor etc.).

Looking back on this time I can see that life was pressurized and we were trapped in an activist pattern. There was evidence of hidden conflict beneath my controlled, professional exterior, occasionally breaking through the surface such as when I left PA and when I lost faith and cut back the team. At the time life seemed mostly OK – sort of normal.

Moving towards authenticity

A little later on, in the summer of 1992, I was reading Peter Block's book *Flawless Consulting* and I was struck by his emphasis on 'being authentic'. The word 'authentic' seemed to ring bells for me, and I realized that authenticity had been missing from my professional life since joining PA and perhaps before then. I felt that, all the time, I had been drawn towards being authentic without quite succeeding and never quite putting into words that authenticity was a value or goal for me. I felt that others viewed my feeble attempts at authenticity as being foolish, naive, 'not the way we do business'. With a colleague, I wrote an article for *Management Consultancy Magazine* which was eventually published in October 1992 under the title 'How to Spot a Faker'.

In writing this I recognized a risk: I was highlighting a gap that still existed between my thinking and my doing. In other words, I was not yet 'walking the talk'. But I suppose I thought that by stating this standard publicly, I would find it easier to become authentic in my professional life. Following publication there were a few kind words from colleagues, there was at least one puzzled client but otherwise not much reaction. My problem then was that I did not know if I was being authentic or not, and my intuition said I was not: my non-authentic habits were deeply ingrained.

All the time, as a consultant, I have felt a strong motivation to discover a theme that can add strength to my consulting work, ensuring survival, continuing viability and sustainability. I wanted to understand why clients engaged me, what the longer-term results of our work together really were and how best to create value with, and for, the client. After the 'authenticity' insight I felt I was moving slowly in this direction but not fast enough. The business still felt fragile although the fee income was satisfactory. I was finding things confusing, and this is why I started to keep a diary.

Starting the diary

I started making daily entries on my laptop in January 1993. Soon I found myself recording quite remarkable events that might previously have passed in the background, almost below consciousness. The diary quite quickly began to give me a greater sense of control and confidence. I suppose this was why I kept it going. From time to time I would look back at earlier entries and notice themes or patterns in my behaviour. I also started to notice moods. I noticed how a mood of optimism or pessimism could colour everything and how long the mood would endure. I found that once I expressed worries and concerns in the diary, I often became free of them. Those that persisted I could sort of interrogate, find their roots and then identify some positive actions or intentions that would propel me forward, out of my previous sense of 'stuckness'. I noticed how there is a spill-over from home life into work and vice versa.

Self-deception was pointless and I adopted a stance of self-criticism and a brutal honesty. I also tried to give expression to positive feelings and higher intentions. I discovered that emotional honesty – the step beyond intellectual honesty – was something to strive for.

Nourished by many conversations

As I write this I'm aware that the diary activity sounds lonely and isolated. I actually found it a brief and pleasant interlude in a busy and gregarious life. My dialogue with the diary helped me to take in and transform many pressures and problems that life throws up, instead of ignoring them. It also added a positive stimulus and productive direction to life. Through the diary-based learning, I felt less fixed in my viewpoint, freed from some of my prejudices and able to see reality more clearly with all its inherent complexity and contradictions. It was like a heightened awareness.

As a consultant and as a 'thinker', the diary was not the only thing that nourished my practice and my learning. Each day in the process of chasing business, doing work and in living my home life, I was engaged in a whole series of conversations. Being married to a management consultant brings with it a diverse range of conversation topics from the corporate (for example, what do we think about business process re-engineering, total quality management, ISO 9000, downsizing and so on?) to the more personal (for example, what do we think about family, friends, relationships, stress, divorce, medicine, alcoholism, obesity, health, illness, death, ethics and so on?). The diary was a 'conversation with myself' that was nourished by many 'conversations with others', both at home and at work.

The helicopter view

How does the method work? I don't know exactly. The diary encourages a rich interaction between one's internal and external worlds, between what is subjective and objective, between personal and work life, between feelings and facts. It registers uncomfortable feelings and turns them into positive learning. It reminds me of my values. It challenges assumptions I am making. It puts me in touch with my feelings and the emotional undercurrent to life but at the same time, paradoxically, it fosters an emotional detachment so that, instead of being locked within problems, I can see myself and the problems from the outside. The diary reduces my tendency to deny or ignore what is happening. It helps me see reality more clearly. This is sometimes called gaining the 'helicopter view'.

Awareness of a pattern or a problem often seems to be enough, change occurring spontaneously and unconsciously following the moment of awareness. This is supported by many experts in this field including, for example, Timothy Gallwey in The Inner Game method. The diary method's power arises perhaps from the way that it deepens and extends awareness, thus accelerating personal change.

By the end of 1994, the diary contained some very interesting material that I realized could be of interest to a wider audience. There was a theme running through it about 'value' – that is, how I, as a consultant, could create the highest possible value with my clients, what was blocking me from creating greater value and what I was learning about consultancy.

With so many people operating as consultants today, it is clear that there is much more to it than getting the business cards printed and rushing in to offer your expertise. The factor X that distinguishes really effective consulting from the disappointing and ineffective is not, in many cases, 'technical expertise'. Factor X is to do with the client–consultant relationship and the consultant knowing where and how they actually create the most value.

Towards publication

Early in 1995 I met a publisher by chance and began talking about writing a diary-style book that reveals what consultancy is all about. The 'value' theme formed the original title for this book.

Initially I felt uncomfortable about how much of my life and other people's lives to include. So I came up with a few decision rules including:

- Keep it real, specific and detailed.
- No sex (sorry!).
- Seek not to harm or embarrass anyone.
- Change the names of our children but include them as characters.
- Where possible, gain permissions from others referred to but otherwise disguise the context so that people are unrecognizable.

Once I had written an early draft, I gave it to Helen, my wife, to read and comment on. I made some changes and passed the next draft on to several other people to read – both people (clients and colleagues) who feature in the diary and others who are not involved. I made a couple of mistakes, upsetting one person and generating a solicitor's letter from another! I also gained a great deal of feedback which, apart from helping me to shorten, simplify and clarify the book, also strengthened my conviction about the value and the power of the diary method.

From the feedback, most interesting of all was the comment that there is a bigger, overarching theme in the diary beyond 'value'. I was told that, over the period covered by the diary entries, I had been undergoing a personal transition. At the start of the diary I was apparently task-driven and by the end I had the task and the client relationship in balance. In the words of this client:

This diary is the story of a guy who was aloof, over analytical and rather tuned out of relationships. This was what his clients and the situation required of him and he succumbed to it. This diary is about your waking up to life, to relationships and their inherent unpredictability.

As a result of this feedback, I have extended the original idea for the book and I offer it now as an example of 'personal transformation'. What in effect happened was that the search for value (first theme) supported by the diary method produced a personal transformation (second theme).

The diary material presented in Part II has been regrouped and edited down into the five broad phases in the personal transition that I experienced. For each phase there is a reflection or summary of learning. The material in Part III serves as a 'reflection on reflections', building up the themes of value, transformation, learning and performance.

How to use this book

What you can expect to gain

I expect that, by reading this book, you will gain a new yardstick against which to evaluate your business relationships, some new ideas about generating value and some further ideas about transformation and learning.

Those people who have already read the book experienced a range of reactions from the positive:

I enjoyed reading it.

It excites me. It is very courageous.

The book helps make clear what consulting is all about. It is original, a breath of fresh air for people who are bored with conventional texts.

Once I got past the first bit I could not put it down.

I really liked it. It is a *tour de force*, rich and profound. It is a consultant's book, a really rich fruit cake.

I personally would be extremely proud of authoring such a readable and intelligent book.

I liked that you brought in the family and personal experiences. I have the feeling that it is very significant. I found it both intellectually stimulating and emotionally moving at the same time. I feel excited about the possibilities it raises both at work and play.

As a result of reading this it is clearer to me where I am and am not adding value with my clients.

. . . to the concerned, dissatisfied, bemused or confused:

The warts and all nature of this raised my concerns. I did not like some of the warts.

The opening up forces the reader to confront their own illusions, projections, fallacies and prejudices about consultants and consultancy.

People can only stomach so much reality.

I have a slight feeling of snooping, that I should not be reading about your life.

The essence of consultancy is not necessarily something the client wants to be pointed out.

When I got to the bits about your home life my mood changed from an objective and work related mood to sympathy. It would be better if you left these bits out.

We know there is a benefit in speaking the truth but in the goldfish bowl of the public domain be careful, sensitive wording is important . . . but then there is the risk of losing the edge of authenticity.

You lack humility. You are putting yourself at the centre of the universe.

The degree of honesty and openness could work against you: it does not always present you in the best possible light.

Clients want to believe in your competence. This could dent your image. Clients don't want to know the truth about you and your personal life, until they get to know you better.

Some of the commentaries are false in their clarity - just like consultancy itself is. Consultancy promises you can plan and deliver something out there in the future, independently of the changing environment/context. You can't.

Possible reactions, feelings and projections

Clearly, the book can stir different reactions in different readers. As a writer I cannot take responsibility for the feelings and reactions you might have. For any feeling that arises, I would ask you: 'Where is the feeling?', 'Is the feeling in the book, or is it in you?' Reading this material can be a little like looking in the mirror. The meanings that emerge for you from the text are a result of your interpretations. A whole range of projections and prejudices might present themselves but, if you use the exercises and work with them, the material can help reveal your assumptions, your contradictions and your values. This can be a rich source of learning for you.

As you read it, you might feel you are being challenged to bring more of yourself into business and to expect others to do the same. This thinking runs counter to many business cultures, and you might find it uncomfortable. If you do, then I hope that you are able to transform the discomfort into some kind of positive learning.

Ways of reading it

So far people have taken quite different approaches to reading the book – for example:

I kept a pad beside me all the time, I was looking for nuggets and noting them down. . . .

I keep it on the car seat and read it in between client meetings. . . .

I read it thoroughly. I found myself sitting up in bed reading it until 12.30 at night. . . .

I read as much of it as I could, I'm a slow reader. . . .

I just read the bits that relate to me. . . .

I started dipping in but now I want to read it again from front to back. . . .

Each section I read makes me think about something I am experiencing in my business life. . . .

Things sort of emerge from it. I want to start it again, then I'll notice different things. . . .

The diary section in Part II is structured into:

- daily entries
- frequent first-level commentaries on entries with a focus on the 'value' theme
- second-level commentaries at the end of the five phases, with a focus on the 'transformation' theme
- an exercise at the end of each phase to encourage active reader participation.

I invite you, as a reader, to remember the Matsushita curse, not to be seduced into passive voyeuristic mode but to treat reading this as a learning opportunity by:

- being self-reflective and active in your use of the book
- using a notepad to record your feelings and reactions as you read
- 'owning' and exploring your reactions, not projecting these on to the book or the writer
- using the exercises and questions to develop your 'helicopter view'
- reading the section in Part III on learning to support your own future reflective learning.

I wish you an enjoyable, challenging and worthwhile read!

Part II
THE DIARY

Phase 1: Fall

The journey begins with a short, sharp shock, which ended a longstanding business relationship.

Thursday 28 January 1993

Earlier today Edward my co-trainer and Hans, a middle-aged German, had clashed. I had heard both Edward's and Hans' sides of the story and expected nothing more.

Then it's midnight, after the course dinner and the customary pint(s), Madonna is blaring from the jukebox and I'm sitting at a table with Edward and our client (who commissioned around 80 per cent of my work last year).

Edward is telling me Hans must leave the programme. Edward insists he is being balanced and objective. I say the dialogue with Hans is not yet complete and I have some data that has not been considered. When I start to describe what Hans has told me, Edward is interrupting. I stop him and plough on. He is not really listening and tries to defeat each point in a debate. I stress that we need to share data and not to make any decisions tonight. Edward said I was implying his judgement was out.

I can remember holding the table and shouting at Edward. I could feel my heart thumping. My hands were shaking, and afterwards I was unable to speak for what seemed like ages. I had become very angry and heated. My blood had boiled. I do not know how apparent this was.

I'm not used to being angry and I am slightly scared by this incident. What is worse, Edward and I were breaking a consultancy rule by having a fight in front of our client.

Value through honesty

In this incident I was being totally honest. I was expressing my true feelings. If a consultant is not honest and willing to express both true facts and true emotions before the client, is he really trustworthy? Until this incident I had kept my emotions hidden and separate from my professional life.

Value through being principled

The proposed removal of Hans compromised my principles. I felt that Hans' career could be harmed by this. I was not able to sit quietly by and condone something that seemed wrong.

Value through self-control

I lost my self-control. I was frustrated that my point of view was not listened to. If I behaved like this all the time I would be unemployable as a consultant. What client would trust me to operate in emotional or fraught situations? The frustration had probably been building up over months and years and finally demanded expression. In this incident my lack of self-control destroyed thousands of pounds of possible future fee income for me. Correspondingly, I lost the opportunity to create further value with and for this client.

Tuesday 2 February 1993

Edward came straight to the point: he did not want to talk about what happened and we needed to end our business relationship. The work we had already contracted to do we should complete but we would not be contracting to do any more work together.

I felt very surprised and a little confused. Helen was helpful in talking it through. She says it is probably a good thing as Edward and I never really saw eye-to-eye and I was getting too much training work (which requires time away from home) through him anyway. Last year a high proportion of my fees did arise from our collaboration but we'll just have to see how events unfold.

Edward and I were co-facilitating a teambuilding workshop in the Midlands today, with a hotel company client. He was totally correct and professional. We're off to a good start but we'd better tread carefully. When the sensitivities with my colleague are so heightened I feel as though I'm negotiating a minefield.

CO-FACILITATING

Value through professional detachment

If we had pulled out of this workshop, we (around 15 clients/participants and both consultants) could all have suffered. It was just about possible to retreat to a cool professional distance from my colleague, but this probably mirrored itself in interactions with and between participants thus severely restricting the value available to the client. How can anything really positive or exciting emerge when we're both being so tight, formal and guarded?

Wednesday 3 February 1993

The workshop ended OK and, after a brief discussion, Edward and I went our separate ways.

Reflections on the fall phase

What was really going on?

The Hans incident touched a nerve. It sparked an explosion between us. This had never happened to me before, and I felt totally out of control and confused.

What is my theory about why?

I can only speak for my side.

Edward and I had always had our differences, and these had often helped us in our work. There are interpersonal style differences: he expresses his view strongly whereas I sometimes hide rather than expose my embryonic views to the fierce battlefield of debate. I prefer my ideas to be given oxygen, to be nurtured and coaxed more gently into life. Despite apparently overcoming previous difficulties together, I suspect we were both carrying secret frustrations or resentments.

We had frequently worked in situations where there was a lot at stake for me, for Edward and for the client. Edward said he found me anxious. This might have been because I was very task-driven, competitive, results-oriented and controlled. My anxiety fuelled his anxiety.

The article I had published the previous October in *Management Consultancy Magazine* about 'authenticity' represented a belief that, to be totally trustworthy, a consultant must be able to be themselves with the client. The best consultant is a 'non-anxious presence', but I was not: I was still anxious and controlled. Writing this article was a kind of antidote to my habitual style, but it was slow-acting.

I think the Hans incident was just the straw that broke the camel's back. The pressure had been building beneath the surface for a long time. The incident was a step towards authentic operating, but it did so much damage that I was pitched into a survival mode: get some new business or go out of business.

REFLECTIONS

EXERCISE

EXERCISE: LOCATING FEELINGS

Previous readers have found that reading this diary produces a range of feelings and reactions.

1 Which of the following feelings have you experienced so far while reading this book?

Happiness	☐	Envy	☐
Arrogance	☐	Complacency	☐
Sadness	☐	Boredom	☐
Surprise	☐	Worry	☐
Anger	☐	Loneliness	☐
Keen interest	☐	Security	☐
Vulnerability	☐	Sympathy	☐
Fear	☐		

2 Use your own words to describe your mood or feelings as you were reading this first phase of the diary?

3 Reflect on the questions :

- 'Where is the feeling?'
- 'Is the feeling in the writing or is it in you?'
- 'Where does the feeling come from?'

Make a brief note of your conclusions.

4 What is your usual way of dealing with uncomfortable or happy feelings?

5 How do you think you can make use of your feelings and reactions as you continue reading, to support your own reflective learning?

Phase 2: Fight back

FIGHT BACK

The journey continues with a couple of small assignments with new clients and then an enquiry from another new client for an important piece of work. There were several months of heavy workload and pressure which spilt over into home life. During this period I was continually struggling to regain control.

Friday 5 February 1993

Set off early for a breakfast meeting at Burford Bridge Hotel outside Dorking at the foot of Box Hill. Lovely small hotel in picturesque setting. Meeting with Account Director from advertising agency. Young chap, fitted the yuppie stereotype, brand victim, living fast. My meeting was his second that day, the first was at 7am with a client in Dorking.

A great British breakfast, with eggs and bacon followed by toast and marmalade. Somehow, between mouthfuls, we managed to talk. I am being asked to facilitate a one-day brainstorming workshop with the board of a cross-Channel ferry company.

Why am I chasing a one-day brainstorming workshop? It is hard to justify the fee cost for pre-briefing, the day itself and the follow-up needed. I found myself complying, agreeing, being nice. Keen to get the work I suppose.

PROJECT PLAN	w/c 1/2	8/2	13/2	22/2	CLIENT: FERRY CO (AD AGENCY)
1. BRIEFING	▌				
2. DESIGN & PREPARE		⌐┄┄┄┄┐			
3. RUN AWAYDAY			▌		
4. FOLLOW-UP MEETING				▌	

BRAINSTORMING PROJECT

Value through offering your expertise

The Account Director needed an experienced facilitator and he had found one.

Value through scoping and planning

We identified the client needs (both the advertising agency and ferry company), drafted out a workshop programme, allocated responsibilities and planned the way forward.

Value through standing your ground

I felt as though I was complying, fitting in to the client's preconceived ideas as to what was needed. I was unsure about whether I could trust the client. I did not pursue this because I wanted the job to go ahead. I now realize that if I know my own mind, stand my ground, require answers to my questions and trust myself, then some

SURE. YES, OK. ABSOLUTELY! IF YOU LIKE. WHY NOT?

COMPLYING

enquiries will go away but those that remain will gain more from my contribution. The relationship, being soundly based, is likely to endure for longer.

Wednesday 16 February 1993

Completed a leadership and teamworking course with managers from a London local authority. It was tough due to their turbulent context: competitive tendering, ethnic issues, ambitious senior management and cost pressures. Groups were often in storming mode, and anger surfaced easily.

I ran an exercise where Planners and Doers in a task become very angry with one another. The Doers got angry at first for being ignored while the Planners made their plans. Later the Planners became angry because the Doers decided to ignore their instructions. The situation became deadlocked and I stepped in as facilitator to help to unblock things. It seemed that at the heart of this lay a feeling on both sides of not being valued, appreciated or recognized.

PROJECT PLAN						CLIENT: LOCAL AUTH	
	SEP	OCT	NOV	DEC	1993 JAN	FEB	MAR
1. BRIEFING	I						
2. DESIGN + PLANNING					I I		
3. RUN WORKSHOPS (FOR TOP 100)						I I I	
4. FOLLOW-UP MEETING							I

LOCAL AUTHORITY PROJECT

Value through surfacing conflict

Before the course, project groups had become bogged down. During the course the tutors worked first with these groups, asking each person in turn to express their experience of being in the group. Once things had been said you could sense the atmosphere getting lighter – the log jam was unblocking. Then the groups were mixed up and blockage occurred again in the Planner/Doer exercise. We were able to see how conflict had arisen and how it could be dealt with.

THE PLAN IS NO GOOD!

DOER

THEY WON'T FOLLOW THE PLAN

PLANNER

SURFACING CONFLICT

Monday 22 February 1993

Lunch at central London ad. agency as follow-up meeting to the ferry company brainstorming workshop. Adland is still different from life as the rest of us know it, even post-recession.

MTV was blaring out in the reception area. Gorgeous girls lazily occupy the reception desk without appearing to work at all. A telephone is available for free use by waiting visitors. Uncorked wine was ready to drink with our lunch although we choose tea. My account director client told me he was going filming in LA the week after next.

He was pleased with my work and led me to expect further facilitation enquiries from him.

Value through professional facilitation

I learned that participants had fun and were pleased with the outcome of the workshop. They acknowledged the value they gained from having a 'professional facilitator'. Some of the ideas produced have since been implemented, helping to keep the ferries attractive since the Chunnel has opened.

Value through involving the power figure

Unfortunately the client MD had to leave for an emergency meeting just one hour after the start of the workshop and, by being absent, did not 'own' the results. Since he holds the power to implement, the ideas produced had to be 'sold' to him. With hindsight I should have briefed the power figure more carefully beforehand and contracted clearly with him about his involvement (that is, no phone calls or interruptions or the meeting is called off).

Tuesday 9 March 1993

Enquiry from Joe, an old colleague at PA Consulting, demanding all of my available time over the next six weeks to develop a training course for a healthcare company.

Sounds interesting. Here is
the gist of it:

PROJECT PLAN	M93 JAN	F	M	A	M	J	J	A	S	O	N	D	J	CLIENT: HEALTHCARE CO. 1994
1. TOP 300 MANAGERS	▨													
2. TRAINING 50,000 STAFF					DESIGN	DELIVER							⊿	
3. CEO RETIRES													✳	

NEW MEGA PROJECT

- Following a merger of
  two companies, the
  client is seeking to
  achieve a common work
  culture, across all
  geographical and
  business sectors, worldwide.
- Expectations have been raised amongst the top 300
  managers at a recent conference that education will
  be rolling out from 10 May onwards.
- The CEO is keen to complete the programme rollout to
  over 50,000 staff worldwide before he retires in 12
  months.
- The education so far has been poorly delivered, boring —
  disastrous in fact. We need quickly to develop
  education which is understandable, motivational and
  delivering real skill.
- We will train 40 or so trainers who each will train 7
  other trainers who each train 7 facilitators who will
  actually use what they learn with groups of people in
  workplaces such as factories, laboratories and offices.

Getting the job hinges mainly on my availability over
the next few weeks to get immersed in it. I sense a great
deal of urgency and pressure. I am beginning to get
anxious about whether I have the capacity to handle all
of this work if it comes my way. Next step is a meeting at
company HQ on Thursday.

Value through being available
At the enquiry stage it is my availability and my
willingness to proceed to the next stage that creates value
for the client, provided, of course, that I am the right
person for this work.

Thursday 11 March 1993

Meeting at healthcare company. Impressive cluster of buildings with well laid-out paved spaces between them.

Joe met me in reception and took me upstairs. He introduced me first to Richard ('an ally') designated as the sponsor for our project. We then all three went in to 'do the business' with Stewart ('budget holder in charge of the change programme who reports to the Chief Executive'). I was warned that he is a tough negotiator and I felt a little like a lamb being led to slaughter!

I was told: 'Forget it if you planned to take any holiday. If you have any other client work to do, you had better get used to working all night and all weekend. Expect a lot of "piss and hysteria" surrounding this programme'. I was shocked by the direct, antagonistic style. I was tempted to say 'If that's how you feel, no thanks'. But I restrained myself and switched into a kind of survival/coping mode

I learned about a fixed delivery date of 10 May for a pilot five-day course (that we were to design and deliver) to enable mass training in June/July, leading to around 1,000 facilitators trained by year end.

Afterwards Joe and Richard told me I held up well, coming out with a good fee rate and making only a small concession on travel expenses. I was told that the 10 May deadline was non-negotiable.

The job was confirmed. It is larger than I first expected with more extension possibilities, worth perhaps 25% of this year's turnover and taking up all my available time for the next three months. My mind-set shifted 180 degrees in an instant from 'how to get more work' to 'how to survive overwork, how not to neglect existing clients and how to manage cash flow'.

Value through being responsive
From this contracting meeting, the client gained a willing, compliant and competent consultant to support the corporate change programme. The client was himself complying with urgency imposed by the CEO and a high level of responsiveness was expected from everyone.

Value through challenging

I was off-balance from the browbeating for a few critical moments and forgot my standards of good consulting practice. I suppose I was also hungry for the work and the income. There was no real invitation to contribute or challenge the *fait accompli* presented. The client gained my compliance but did not really engage my full intelligence or motivation. Much of what occurred later was predictable and can be traced back to the absence of challenge at this contracting stage.

Friday 12 March 1993

Whenever my work gets busy Helen and I fall out. As far as I can make out, it affects Helen like this: I assume she will cover the kids and the household responsibilities because she only works three days per week. Helen then feels taken for granted and undervalued. When this happens she becomes abrasive and hard to talk to. She develops a heightened sense of self-righteousness and I do too. Communication breaks down.

DISSONANCE

So what is the problem with this? Well, it is a big problem for me. I experience inner discomfort and stress. I feel shitty inside. I find it hard to be natural with anyone when I feel like this. I feel right, hard done by and misunderstood. I feel undervalued. It is as if by some curious invisible mirror, I experience what Helen experiences: being undervalued and unsupported.

Do I have to live through each job against a background of conflict and turmoil? I do not know the answer and I wish I did.

Thursday 18 March 1993

Meeting at healthcare client on the second floor of the light and stylish HQ building, with Joe and Richard (our sponsor), to discuss the project plan.

Meeting hijacked into a full-scale course design meeting. Richard had to put a draft course programme urgently to Stewart and the CEO for discussion. As a result we ran out of time and Joe had to leave. Richard and I ran on until after 6pm when I was supposed to meet the kids. I faced a clash of loyalties but resolved it by drawing the meeting abruptly to a close and going, albeit 30 minutes late, to fulfil my parental role.

Value through adaptability

I was irritated that the project was already out of control: we were doing the work before the plan had been agreed. The client gained value from our responsiveness to a new emerging priority. If we had insisted on sticking to the original (planning) agenda, Stewart and Richard would have had to cobble something together for the CEO with the risk of setting up false expectations.

Monday 22 March 1993

Outside the hotel restaurant.
Waiter: 'I am sorry, I don't want to be rude but you cannot eat here in your jeans.'
Customer: 'We will find somewhere else to eat, then.'
Waiter: 'I am sorry, but we do not let people in dressed like that.'
Customer: 'Do you never make an exception?'
Waiter: 'This is difficult for me. Yes, OK, I will this time.'

This exchange taught me something about assertion. I would have been inclined to accept the house rule rather than seek an exception. The customer stuck to his guns. He is paying the bill after all, and the rule seems archaic.

Tuesday 23 March 1993

Woke up at 7am in the hotel room. Entire day spent working with Joe on the project at Frederick's Hotel in Maidenhead, addressing some fundamental questions.

Q. Who are the course materials for and how will they be used?

A. For 52,000 people, reaching out from trainers to facilitators to work groups in factories, laboratories and offices throughout the world. Too many people to know individually: a huge range of talents, experience, cultures and motivations just in the trainer group.

To avoid confusion and dilution, we must be specific both with the facilitators and with the trainers. First we will describe clearly for the facilitator what to do in the workplace. We decided to produce a detailed 'Route Map'.

Secondly we will give clear instructions for the trainers. We settled on a style which says 'ask participants X', 'explain to participants Y'. This is better than a script and encourages the trainers actively to think about and plan their sessions.

We also developed a list of World Class Training Principles to help us achieve an understandable, motivational design that delivers real skill.

I asked Joe how he had managed to get to the centre of this huge change programme in the four months since he joined the company. He said by being a catalyst, giving direct and impartial feedback to people. So, for example, in a long tedious meeting where people are skirting round the important issues, when he is asked for his view, he will say 'I feel we are skirting round the issues and not really getting anywhere in this meeting'.

The effect of this style of intervention is apparently very powerful.

Value through building a shared concept

We achieved clarity about the shape of the materials we will produce, freeing us to fill in the details and move ahead towards our deadline of 10 May.

Value through addressing concerns

I had concerns that were not easy to express about the decisions we took. Being directive to the facilitators and trainers in a facilitation course could create confusion, resistance and inhibit learning about the true nature and power of facilitation.

With hindsight we needed to pause, express our

models of facilitation and make sure the materials, both Route Map and Trainer Guide, were fully compatible. We did not have time. I went along with the decisions without being fully satisfied.

Value through being a catalyst
I want to be a catalyst!

Thursday 25 March 1993

IMMERSION

Work continues on the project at Frederick's. We are getting overloaded: the work seems to be expanding. We are developing four courses now instead of one. That is why we have been working 12–14 hour days.

Why not bring some other consultants in to help us? Joe and I are working very effectively together and are reluctant to spoil this. With the 10 May deadline in mind and difficulty in finding the right person and bringing them up to speed, extending the team feels like a big and unnecessary risk.

Travelled home late afternoon. Completed annual review discussion with Rosemary, my assistant. Picked kids up from childminder. Took them to Burger King for tea. Babysat while Helen attended nursery school parents induction meeting.

Value through feeling special
Our conversation about extending the team reconfirmed our satisfaction with ourselves and each other. It made us both feel special, gifted, rare and valuable. But I noticed how easily this spills over into arrogance and contempt for others. It feels real, but it is a kind of fool's paradise.

Value through immersion
We were learning to work very quickly and effectively together. There was a rapport: we seemed to think the same way. But at the same time I was concerned that we were developing a fortress mentality: respecting and understanding each other very well but distancing

ourselves from the rest of the world. By comparison others seemed ill-informed or incompetent. I remember experiencing this feeling years ago in PA Consulting.

Going home was like breaking out from a very intense immersion – reconnecting with the world outside.

Value through monitoring workload

Becoming overloaded is unpleasant. It can happen quite suddenly: two days ago there was little sign of it. Two weeks ago I had virtually nothing to do.

Friday 26 March 1993

Entry meeting first thing with HR Director at hotel company HQ near Heathrow. Meeting went well. Client was interested in the article I had written on being authentic with the client ('How to Spot a Faker', Management Consultancy Magazine, October 1992).

Returned to Frederick's to work for the rest of the morning.

Afternoon back to my office to continue the work. Had tea with family then took children and Helen's father for a drink before setting off with Helen for a late-night flight to Malaga.

PROJECT PLAN — CLIENT: HOTEL COMPANY A

	MAR	APR	MAY	JUN	JUL	AUG
1. ENTRY MEETING	▨					
2. DESIGN + PREP + INTERVIEWS				▨		
3. FACILITATE TEAMBUILDING WORKSHOP					▨	
4. FOLLOW-UP MEETING					▨	

TOP TEAMBUILDING PROJECT

Value through clarifying a need

The entry meeting with hotel client produced value by clarifying a need/opportunity, defining a two-day top team workshop to meet the need and agreeing the next steps.

Value through being stretched

I was operating in overdrive, my feet hardly touching the ground (from home to hotel client back to healthcare client back to home then off to Spain). I usually prefer to be less activist with more reflective time, but I did enjoy the feeling of being stretched and in demand.

Value through PR
The magazine article was copied by my client to each of his director colleagues as a way of selling me in.

Value through a public declaration
The article was about being authentic. This provides a rigorous test of my ability to be myself, not to pretend or role play.

Saturday 27 March 1993

Arrived at villa at 3am. Our four friends who arrived yesterday were waiting up to toast our arrival with sparkling wine. I felt very happy and extremely relaxed. Slept through to around noon. Helen and I joined the other four in bright, warm sunshine to eat our boiled eggs.

The freedom of this break felt very strange after six years of life built around the children. This was the first time Helen and I had spent together away from the kids in three years. The other two couples were at a similar life stage. There was a vacuum without the children. It felt good not to have to do anything, but at the same time we did not want to waste the weekend.

It felt like we had left, say, the army and were needing a new structure to life. The others described their previous day's routine: wake up late, take breakfast on verandah above pool, walk on beach, have tapas lunch and wine, return to sunbathe and read by pool, take two-hour siesta, wake up and get ready, go into Marbella for restaurant meal, drink wine, go to bed late. Helen and I were happy to fall in with this.

Unfortunately, in spite of the weather, the weekend in Spain was marred for me. Late on Saturday night, Helen volunteered to drive home and being unfamiliar with the left-hand-drive hire car in a narrow street drove into another car by mistake. I was in the passenger seat and

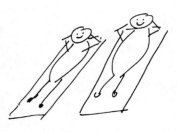

BRIGHT WARM SUNSHINE

yelled 'Stop!'. We did – just in time. The mirror was already jammed against the green paintwork of a new Range Rover parked on our right. I yanked our mirror from its mount leaving us free to drive away without doing any significant damage to the other car.

Helen drove on and gained enough confidence to get us safely home. The others all expressed thanks and support to Helen for getting us back safely, leaving me well and truly out in the cold. Helen had lost face and blamed me! At the time of writing this, three days later, I still feel under a cloud. Helen and I have not yet made up or forgiven each other.

Value through work /life balance

When there is background pressure at work, this can spill over and interfere with private life. The reverse is also true.

Tuesday 30 March 1993

Back to Frederick's first thing in the morning, fighting through the traffic around Heathrow and the M4.

Sticky telephone conversation with Helen over a date in May when she is in Manchester giving a talk. She needs to stay overnight and wanted me to look after the kids. It is in the week commencing 10 May and so clashes with the climax of all the healthcare company work.

Joe and I had a very memorable session which produced a model to integrate our ideas about facilitator/consultant development. It is a set of lopsided concentric circles. We called it the 'basketball model'. How did we produce it? First, Joe asked me about how I take care of my own development and I asked him about his development plan. We were both quite candid. The ensuing discussion was animated. We uncovered important connections between our own experience and the content of the course.

On another topic, I realized today that, when a consultant takes on an assignment, they need to contract or agree the terms with their line boss and

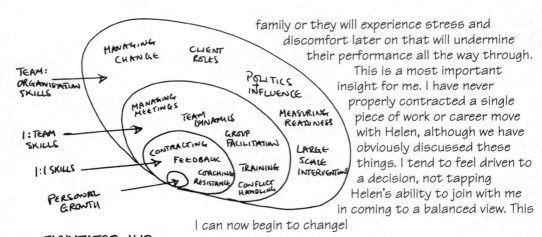

FACILITATOR AND CONSULTANT DEVELOPMENT MODEL

family or they will experience stress and discomfort later on that will undermine their performance all the way through. This is a most important insight for me. I have never properly contracted a single piece of work or career move with Helen, although we have obviously discussed these things. I tend to feel driven to a decision, not tapping Helen's ability to join with me in coming to a balanced view. This I can now begin to change!

Value through co-creation

Today Joe and I created together a unique new property in the 'basketball model'. I became interested in how creative our session was, how it produced a tangible and original product from thin air and how this represented the creation of unique value from a consulting relationship. I have since noticed this happening more and more in consulting work. I call it a 'generative conversation'.

Value through recontracting

I realized that my home life (the clash of dates, my inadequate contracting with Helen over my work commitments and the hangover from our fall-out in Spain) is constantly in the background, sapping my energy and distracting me. This is due to taking on the new commitment (this project) without consulting about, and recontracting, my existing commitments. I am taking the strain and short-changing others both at work and home.

Thursday 15 April 1993

Last night Helen and I argued. Today I plodded on with the project at Maidenhead. So far we have completed one day of the course design. Joe is leaving me free to get on with the job, which I appreciate, but is getting diverted himself: keeping his real job going and dealing with a mountain of other arrangements. In his own words he is 'running on empty'.

The long day was capped with an evening meeting, conducted over dinner, with our sponsor, Richard. At this meeting we let him know all of our concerns. He dealt with each one coolly in turn, like batting back difficult balls in a game of cricket.

My main concern was that working this intensely is harmful and should not be expected. Richard batted this back to me by attacking the way I had scheduled my personal time on the project. Joe came quickly to my support, reminding Richard that I had, at short notice, freed up all my time for this project.

The outcome was I made an agreement with Richard that after we have completed this piece of work:

EXPRESSING CONCERNS

- Richard will brief me on another course design needed for the autumn
- the working days will be shorter
- I will not usually contract to five full days on a project in any week.

After the meeting, I felt exhausted but satisfied.

Value through expressing concerns
Until this point I felt we were sinking. Richard's batting-back style made it difficult for me to express my concerns. Once these were expressed, however, the conversation lifted me up again. The taking of responsibility by the sponsor was key to this. When working under great pressure, a relationship in which such honesty is possible is needed with the sponsor or power figure.

Friday 16 April 1993

The air seems to have cleared since the argument with Helen on Wednesday night. Helen has booked a babysitter and we are going out for dinner. It feels like a big weight has been lifted from my shoulders.

Sunday 9 May 1993

Arrived ten minutes late at 5.10pm. As I am writing this, it is 6.45pm and Joe has still not arrived. Did he get back from his conference in Bangkok? Is he jet-lagged or delayed by some other crisis? Will I have to run the course alone tomorrow?

He finally appeared around 7.15pm. His flight back from Bangkok had been delayed by two days! He had seen his family for only four hours at the weekend before coming back to work.

Monday 10 May 1993

The big day which we have been leading up to since the project started in March: the proof of the pudding.

It turned out to be difficult. The group of around 20 participants were trainers drawn from all parts of the business. They had suffered many boring training sessions together. Their mood was quiet – sort of gently hostile.

PROJECT PLAN	M93 JAN	F	M	A	M	J	J	A	S	O	N	D	J
											CLIENT: HEALTHCARE CO.		1994
1. TOP 300 MANAGERS	▨												
2. TRAINING 50,000 STAFF				DESIGN	DELIVER								
3. CEO RETIRES													✳

NEW MEGA PROJECT

We began with a warm-up exercise. One participant's anger boiled over: he could not bear the time-wasting, he just wanted to get on with it. I don't remember exactly what we did but we faced the problem, the participant apologized and the course continued.

Five participants were travelling from the US and when the course started at 9.30am they had still not arrived. We did not want them to disrupt the opening so my job was to hold on to them when they arrived, update them on what they had missed and contract with them about their role and contribution during the course. They arrived and were finally ready to join the course around lunchtime.

One participant wanted to leave the course for a prior appointment and return later. We explained that if you leave, you don't return because of the disruptive effect of re-entry on the rest of the group. He complied, left the course and booked to attend a subsequent course instead. I learned a little later that he was seething about this.

Value through defending the conditions for success

We faced low participant commitment, mild hostility, US late arrivals and other irritants. The situation was fragile. The rules of engagement had to be very clear to prevent the course from disintegrating. Stout defence of the conditions needed for success helped to create value for all. Our job was to be firm and uncompromising.

Tuesday 11 May 1993

At the start of the day the participants rebelled. They wanted to be 'walked through' the course, to debate each session and exercise. In the joining letter we had made clear we expected them to immerse themselves in the course and evaluate later when asked. They were not to come if this was not acceptable. We held them to the contract.

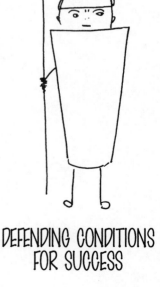

DEFENDING CONDITIONS
FOR SUCCESS

After this conflict, the air was cleared and I felt effective in the facilitator role.

Another critical point arose late in the day when we were all tired. The discussion became negative; the energy dissipated from the group.

Value through firmness
The rebellion could have scuppered the course. It needed to be handled with firmness and sensitivity. Participants were first allowed to express their concerns, then reminded of the reasons for doing the course and the terms on which they were present. This cleared the air and we moved on with renewed energy.

Value through monitoring group energy
Participants were really enjoying learning through immersion in the method. But when they became tired, they nearly gave up at a simple obstacle. It was dangerous to press on. You must stay aware of the group's energy level.

Value through realistic expectations of participants
Don't expect people to behave as self-motivated adults when they have become used to childlike dependency, being manipulated by force, pressure and fear to induce their compliance.

Wednesday 12 May 1993

After a good day of facilitating, I went home in the evening to pick the kids up from the childminder and put them to bed while Helen was in Manchester giving a talk to the British Computer Society.

I was pleased that I went home. I find myself increasingly uncomfortable that normal life for Tom and Georgia does not include me because I am away working. I tested this by asking Tom whether he would prefer me to be at home more and us have less money or vice versa. Tom replied that he wants the money and doesn't mind if I'm away!

This confirmed my fears and privately I resolved to spend more time with him in the week.

Thursday 13 May 1993

The course dinner took place in the mansion situated within the grounds of the training centre. Traditionally a time for letting off steam, this opportunity was much needed after an intense and tiring week.

Around 25 of us were seated at a long rectangular table, enjoying good food and wine, in the oak-panelled room overlooking beautiful manicured lawns when someone mentioned that our visitor, a senior manager, planned to give us a talk using an OHP. I muttered my concern to the person next to me: 'Surely he can't be serious?'. The proposal seemed at odds with the mood of the group. But I was still surprised at the bizarre behaviour that followed.

He got up, tested the projector and launched in with slide after slide packed with hard-to-read statistics: numbers of facilitators nominated in each business sector and geographical area, numbers trained, numbers of projects identified, numbers of projects initiated and so on.

First of all everyone seemed interested. Then a woman from the US decided to sit under the table! She then started inviting others to join her, and a giggling group established itself there while the talk dragged relentlessly on.

One participant finally managed to bring the speech to a close in a most original way. He took a handful of giant tulips from the flower vase, put one in his mouth and walked round the table giving one to each of us, including the speaker. This did get through. The speaker looked foolish holding his tulip, and his flow was interrupted. He showed just a couple more slides then closed.

It's all gone quiet. Must be time to stop.

BIZARRE BEHAVIOUR

Friday 14 May 1993

We closed the course. It went OK. We would both have liked more appreciation for our efforts. The scores on the forms were not bad. There is a bit of rework to do on the materials.

Value through realistic expectations (again!)
The appreciation was mild. I felt rather taken for granted. So much for three months' tough grind! But then I realized that I was delighted simply to get through the week. A weight had been lifted from me, but the participants were now feeling the burden of responsibility themselves. They were concerned about their forthcoming responsibility for training the next tier. Do not expect huge appreciation.

Saturday 15 May 1993

Quiet evening in, watching video. All the tension is now gone between me and Helen. It's happened again: the big pressurized project is over, and we are fine again.

Monday 17 May 1993

Last week I was away on a course, the week before in Tunisia. I'm feeling quite adrift as I have been away from home so much. This week I am meant to be running a residential course in the Midlands but I have decided to drive there and back each day.

Tuesday 18 May 1993

After an exhausting day of training, I worked late to complete the final changes to the training manuals for the healthcare company. I still have not been paid for the last three months' work. I am tired and fed up.

Wednesday 19 May 1993

This is getting too much for me. Via various telephone messages during the day I succeeded in reorganizing my July diary, creating the space to book the hotel company top team workshop. Meanwhile I was running a training course and, after eight hours of exhausting training, I drove for one and a half hours to get home. When I arrived home I prepared a diskette for healthcare client containing the documents they had requested.

EXHAUSTION!

In busy periods consultants tend to neglect enquiries and client servicing, thereby creating the fallow periods. I am not just being greedy trying to do too much work. If I do not sort these things out there will be no work in six weeks or so!

Thursday 20 May 1993

I woke up determined to force the issue with the healthcare company. It's surprising for me to feel so strongly but, after several reminders, our invoices have still not been paid. We need to settle the VAT, and the bank balance will soon be in the red.

I left a note for Rosemary to withhold the corrected manuals and diskette until we receive payment for our outstanding invoices. Then I set off at 7am for the Midlands.

Sure enough, the payment ultimatum put the cat amongst the pigeons. When I phoned during the break from my training course I found that Stewart's assistant had been shouting down the phone at Rosemary. She said, yes, they will pass payment. Rosemary agreed to send materials immediately by courier and did so.

ULTIMATUM

Value through giving an ultimatum

The client was too busy to notice that my needs (in this case, needs for payment) had not been met despite several reminders and promises. This was an attempt to escalate the situation. In that sense it worked, but it was heavy-handed and caused many other problems.

Monday 24 May 1993

PROJECT PLAN

CLIENT: HOTEL COMPANY B

1992 J F M A M J J A S O N D 1993 J F M A M J J A

1. BRIEFING

2. DESIGN MATERIALS

3. DELIVER COURSE(S)

TRAINING GENERAL MANAGERS PROJECT

Early start today. A two-day service delivery course for hotel general managers. It is a new design, so I was on tenterhooks. By the end of the day I knew from comments that the design is working OK.

Evening phone call revealed the extent of the damage my tough stance over payment has caused. Richard's assistant and Stewart's assistant have both been complaining to Stewart about my 'blackmailing' them. Relations are severely strained. The situation is deteriorating, and the quality of my work is being called into question. Stewart is spoiling for a fight and looks as if he may press for a reduction in the bill.

I need to send an apology letter to both assistants and then to tackle the payment issue directly with Richard when he returns. I swallowed my pride, wrote and faxed the apology immediately.

Value through eating humble pie

I seemed to be the villain in this piece: the client was failing to see their responsibility towards me, and I had lost the moral high ground by my ultimatum. The ultimatum itself seemed not to have worked. I had still not been paid. I seemed to have upset everyone: the apology itself upset Rosemary. I understand that, if I ever have to deliver an ultimatum again, it would be better to phone myself rather than giving Rosemary my dirty work.

HUMBLE PIE

Friday 28 May 1993

When I arrived back at the office, to my amazement, there were two cheques waiting, covering all the outstanding money. Helen was working and I picked the kids up early from the childminder. We went home via the bank to pay in the cheques.

Friday 11 June 1993

Tough decision: do we move to Holland? A big chance for Helen in her career with Shell, and it could be exciting to go and live in another country. The downside is uprooting home and kids, letting go of the stability we have worked hard to build. It would interrupt my consulting work. Helen could make more money, but I would earn less for a while.

Keen that we should never live to regret the decision we take, I asked Helen to look at each aspect separately:

- Do you want to go back to work full-time?
- Do you want to work in Holland?
- Do you want the money?

Helen has finally decided she does not want to move. There is a continuing need for her job in the UK, albeit reporting to a new Holland-based boss.

Value through freedom of choice
I expressed my interests. I did not force or pressurize. I trusted Helen to make up her own mind. I reckoned this would lead to the best decision in the end. I was happy with the decision we ultimately reached.

Wednesday 16 June 1993

Helen asked me how much the proposed tree-house will cost. Currently it is over £120. She regards this as excessive. I wanted a large visible project that teaches Tom craft skills and gives the excitement of commissioning something.

While I was explaining this under Helen's critical gaze I felt enthusiasm draining from me. Who really wants to do this? Tom or me? Shouldn't Georgia be as involved as Tom in any project? I began to feel empty, sad and low-spirited as I let go of my pet idea. I get easily attached to a plan, committed to 'delivering'.

I have been short-changing Tom over the last few months of solid work. The tree-house project was my way of paying off the emotional debt. I now realize it would not pay off any debt in Tom's eyes.

Helen suggested we relax a previous stance and offer to buy a pet, such as a hamster, instead of a tree-house and we put the choice to the kids: tree-house or hamster?

TREE-HOUSE PROJECT

Value through taking a critical stance
In this instance, Helen's critical gaze was all that I needed to reconsider my plans.

Thursday 17 June 1993

There is no contest, both children would prefer a hamster.

Wednesday 23 June 1993

Afternoon meeting with Richard, the healthcare client sponsor. Accolades. He was pleased and relieved. The material we developed was rated by customers as excellent, world-class. Evaluation ratings are consistently 4.5 on a five-point scale, some making spontaneous compliments such as 'These are the best courses I have ever been on'. Line managers are succeeding at delivering these courses and, because it is line managers, the courses gain high credibility amongst participants.

I asked what he had learned from working together on the project. There was a long pause, then three points, the first of which was: he would never put anyone else under so much pressure as he put Joe and myself. Good!

He briefed me on a further project he wishes to commission. I was thrilled. He went on to fix a date when four of us can celebrate the completion of the work.

Returned home to a mess where the builders are installing our new kitchen. I noticed that their energy was very low. I made them tea and offered biscuits. They told me Phil couldn't mount the fan, Chris and Eddy hadn't finished the last worktop template and questioned whether it was necessary. Materials were costing them more than expected, eroding their profit from the job. They were tired. I went to the timberyard to buy the final bit of wood needed to mount the fan.

In my opinion, the courses were:

```
1        2        3        4        5
|--------|--------|--------|--------|
DREADFUL         OK              EXCELLENT
                                 (WORLD
                                 CLASS)
```

AVERAGE RATING

ACCOLADES

Value through follow-up

I nearly forgot to ask for this client meeting and, once there, I nearly forgot to ask the critical question about what had the client learned. This is my defensive stance. By asking I accessed real learning for myself. This is the key to identifying and enhancing value. When the answers came back I was energized by the information, and the client was reminded of the value of the work to date.

Value through producing results
The client valued highly the work to date. The programme was rolling out. The results coming back were good. He was vindicated, no longer feeling exposed. He had new power to commission the next project . The next project was commissioned.

Value through awareness of others' needs
After the successful client meeting when my energy was high, I was able to notice the builders' 'stuckness' and was motivated to help them.

Thursday 8 July 1993

Tom is doing fine at school although his report said he would do better if he did not rush to finish everything. It makes me reflect on the pace of our life and how often we tell him to hurry up.

Friday 9 July 1993

A misunderstanding with Helen again over the timing of a workshop next week. We have agreed that one of us should be there always to put the children to bed and get them up in the morning. The problem is we are both due to be away working next Monday evening, Helen in Aberdeen and me on the other side of Oxford.
     Helen is hundreds of miles away and the planes are not at very convenient times, but I am a two-hour car journey away, and as it is up to me to define start and finish times for the workshop programme, I agreed to rearrange schedules and come home to look after the kids.

Monday 12 July 1993

Got up at 5.30am, set off at 6am. Arrived around 8am at a beautiful hotel in a tiny village outside Oxford.

Interviewed the IT Director over breakfast, then facilitated day one of a teambuilding workshop with him and his colleagues. Finished at 4pm. Dashed in car back home. Arrived at 6pm. Helen departed in a taxi at 6.45pm for her two-day workshop in Aberdeen.

I feel highly pressured. These are new clients. This is a very special event – something they have not done before and will not do again for perhaps a year or more. They are paying me a generous fee which I must be seen to earn.

They invited me to dinner and expected me to stay the night. I was profuse in my apologies. It could appear that I am turning away their hospitality. I feel I am short-changing them. Somehow being a parent is not a legitimate excuse. I need to demonstrate a singlemindedness towards the work and not be distracted by any other responsibilities.

What is worse is that this is exactly the kind of work I would like to generate more of: facilitating at board level. Racing between home and client is hardly going to help me do the best quality job or generate repeat business here.

Value through singlemindedness

The pressure on me to be in two places at once was a constant distraction. Helen and I must become even clearer with our diary arrangements and reduce our pace of life to avoid further mistakes.

TOP TEAMBUILDING PROJECT

Tuesday 13 July 1993

Day two of the teambuilding workshop. Set off early again, dropping the kids with Jane on the way. Raced home arriving 1 hour and 15 minutes late. Apologized to childminder.

Value through team discussion and planning

Participants reported learning about themselves and about others. They realized there was a common goal and that they could help each other to succeed. They agreed on key actions and follow-up.

Value through bringing things to a head

One participant with a strong competitive streak received some 'harsh but true' feedback and was smarting from it at the end, but the matter was not brought fully to a head. I was afraid to damage the person or the team by prolonging our work on this issue. Now I realize that the worst that could happen would be the team facing up to its problem and dealing appropriately with it. As it is, the problem is left festering.

Wednesday 14 July 1993

Meeting at a hotel near Gatwick. I lunched with the group of 60 trainers who were undergoing training. I was keen to discover how they were touched by the change programme.

A consultant from Seattle tried to address their concerns. He spoke about Bell Laboratories, Japan, Rover, Honda, General Motors, Toyota. Then the Head of Manufacturing gave a 'business leader's' perspective, underlining the pairing relationship of a leader with a facilitator.

PROJECT PLAN — CLIENT: HEALTHCARE CO. — 1993 JAN F M A M J J A S O N D J 1994
1. TOP 300 MANAGERS
2. TRAINING 50,000 STAFF — DESIGN DELIVER
3. CEO RETIRES — *

NEW MEGA PROJECT

The to and fro of questions and answers showed trainers gripped by real concerns, including a fear of being unsupported by their line managers. They also displayed an energy – a keen desire to succeed. They declared a wish to make a statement to the whole organization.

I heard later that producing the statement was time-consuming and frustrating. When this statement was finally agreed it was bland and disappointing:

We're grateful for the training which has been excellent.
We now want to go on and implement.
We look forward to your continuing support.

The change programme felt real to me today. Each trainer would go on and train seven facilitators. By the end of the year, 1,000 fully trained facilitators would be running workplace improvement projects throughout the world.

Value through listening for concerns
The trainers were fully engaged and striving to deliver value, but their line bosses had not been adequately briefed or trained. The consultant from Seattle and the Head of Manufacturing tried to smooth over this problem instead of listening and bringing it out. They lost some credibility points for this.

Thursday 15 July 1993

Working at Fred's in Maidenhead again. It was good to meet up with Joe again and chat. But we had an urgent task.

A communication event was needed so that each manager throughout the world could gather together their staff and brief them on the change programme. In spite of 4–500 senior managers attending leadership training and 1,000 facilitators who will be ready to run improvement projects, another 50,000 staff spread throughout the business have not got a clue what is going on. They needed to be informed and receptive, otherwise all the previous work might come to nothing.

We need to produce a one-day briefing event for small or large audiences, with simple exercises to bring the change programme to life. A corporate communication manager will be working with us. By the end of next week, the design needs to be 80% complete.

GRIPPED BY REAL
CONCERNS

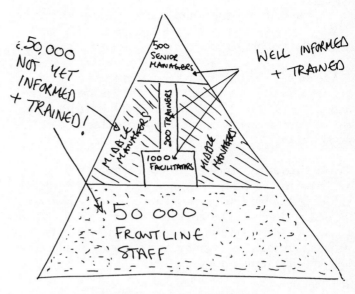

PENETRATION OF MESSAGE

Value through a shared sense of urgency
Having worked intensively together recently, our communication was fast and effective. We shared a common context and understanding. But I noticed I was in a kind of passive mode: listening to understand the need and scoping the work to be done. I still did not feel able to contribute to or challenge the brief. I felt slightly uncomfortable about this but, with the urgency to produce, I barely noticed.

Value through learning reviews
We were highly efficient at production and good at communicating, but there was a simple gap in our learning process. We had not conducted a learning review after the last project together so, without knowing, if we did make any mistakes we were likely to be repeating them.

Tuesday 10 August 1993

I caught a train to Brighton for a meeting at the Grand Hotel with a trainer from Texas. We sat down for a coffee. The foyer was crowded with client people from around the world, here to learn about the leadership role in the corporate change programme. I was infected by a buzz of excitement at the sheer scale and audacity of the overall change programme (although I had not played a part in the development of this particular leadership event).

As I spoke to the trainer, I began to realize that Joe and I were seen as having a 'fortress mentality'. Joe and I had set out to cut through a kind of corporate inertia. We had learned how we could develop excellent education and communication products fast. Our 'rolled-up sleeves', task-oriented mode of working was now alienating others in the trainer community. We were being seen as loose cannons — elitist and self-serving.

Value through listening for harsh truths

Our genuine desire to produce excellent product fast was viewed cynically as being self-serving. This was disappointing to hear. Of course, it was self-serving on one level, but we also felt that it was delivering the highest possible value to the company. Was this some of the 'piss and hysteria' I had been warned about? I felt we could not win. But being willing to listen was an important first step in repairing the damage.

Thursday 26 August 1993

We were in Haworth, West Yorkshire. I got up at 7am with the kids. The sun was shining in the window. After the poor weather recently I wanted to get outdoors. Tom, Georgia and I decided to go straight out before breakfast with paper and pencils to do sketching up on the moors.

We walked past the church and parsonage, through a field, scrambled up on to a rocky hill with a tree. I stood

ON THE ROCKY HILL

behind Georgia to catch her in case she fell back. Tom is OK at climbing on his own now. We had seen some rabbits on the hill in the distance but they hopped away as we approached. When we got to the top Tom was looking for them in all the little crevices between the rocks. We sketched some horses and rocks and the tree. Tom has always enjoyed drawing and, at one point, said he wanted to be a painter when he is grown up. I struggle with drawing. Even Georgia joined in. We were all happy doing this for a time.

After 20 minutes or so we walked on to the Dimple Quarry and did some more drawing. Soon we became hungry and walked back down past the farm into Haworth for breakfast. Georgia fell on the cobbled hill just as we were approaching our cottage. Helen was up and able to comfort and tend to Georgia's cuts.

Value through taking a break
This was a breath of fresh air – literally and metaphorically. It is contact with nature, with life. I don't do it often enough. It changes my mood. It uplifts and re-charges me, bringing my optimism back. I feel this is an essential break from consulting and the corporate jungle. It relaxes me and prepares me for the high levels of concentration I give to my work.

Wednesday 1 September 1993

Tom gave me a pinch and a punch this morning, and I responded with a grunt. It feels like summer is over and life is moving on. I felt low, alone. I let Helen and the kids worry about clearing breakfast. I could not be bothered to offer the usual help. What is the point?

Friday 3 September 1993

Still in a black mood. Up and out early today for an 8am meeting at hotel client in Slough. The kids wanted to have breakfast with me, which lasted all of two minutes –

the time it takes for me to eat a small bowl of Raisin Splitz.

I arrived back after a short meeting around 9.30am to find an empty house and dog-shit footprints on the office carpet. Silently I blamed Helen and the kids but, as it smelt, I decided to clean it up. I soon began to realize, from the position of the prints, that I was the guilty one.

A few minutes later the kids bounced in followed by Helen. Georgia earnestly explained in her three-year old's way that I put dog pooh on the carpet.

Before she went out again Helen fixed me with her eyes, gave me a slow concerned look and a cuddle. This instantly made me feel a little better. Funny thing, feelings. I can't fathom them. Knowing intellectually it is something about being rejected or being included does not help me too much, but the look and the cuddle really did!

Helen has asked me if I want to join them for lunch at Lensbury. I might jog down there to meet them. The physical exercise might lift my black mood.

BLACK MOOD

Wednesday 8 September 1993

I conducted an interview at the healthcare company with a client who is in charge of a breakthrough project which fundamentally redesigns workflow and jobs in the manufacturing division. It seems our previous corporate change programme may be a waste of our time and energy: everyone and everything might be re-engineered out of existence by breakthrough projects. The education, the efforts to communicate and the improvement projects could all be wasted.

The shock of this was reduced when I remembered that there are big problems with implementing breakthrough projects. They cannot easily be implemented except by people in each workplace. A recent article on this theme was entitled 'Getting Turkeys to Vote for Christmas'. This sums it up nicely.

Value through providing education
We had provided education that leads to workplace

projects that involved people in making changes. By contrast, the breakthrough project was secret, over-analytical, remote from the workplace, and no one knew, at this stage, how it could be implemented.

Thursday 23 September 1993

At 8pm Helen came back from her boss's leaving party and I went out to Chutney Mary's, an Anglo-Indian restaurant in King's Road, to celebrate the successful launch of the education programme earlier in the year. There were six of us: Richard, his assistant and Joe I recognized. The other two women had fixed the venue arrangements and helped to prepare piles of course manuals.

PROJECT PLAN	1993 JAN	F	M	A	M	J	J	A	S	O	N	D	CLIENT: HEALTHCARE CO. 1994 J
1. TOP 300 MANAGERS	▨												
2. TRAINING 50,000 STAFF				⌐DESIGN¬	▨▨▨▨DELIVER▨▨▨▨								
3. CEO RETIRES													✱

N̶E̶W̶ MEGA PROJECT

Joe asked each of us for our highs and lows during the project. Joe's low was sacking another consultant. His high was the acceptance of the Route Map by the trainers. My low was the initial browbeating meeting. My high was a trip to the US, marking the end of the pressure. Richard's low was getting rid of yet another consultant who came to observe the pilot course in May. His high was the trainer course in which he said there was a massive release of tension and energy with songs, poetry and hugs. After that he felt the change programme was unstoppable.

He went on to say that, occasionally, someone comes up to him and says the course we developed needs fundamental change. He asks them to be specific and they say things like, 'I want to miss out slide 6b, spend more time on step 4.2 and improve the look of another slide'. Richard says, 'OK, fine, do it!'.

Value through celebrating completion
This was overdue. We really needed more of this earlier: a simple learning review at the end of each meeting and

each project phase and a celebration sooner while we could still feel the joy of accomplishment. There were a few laughs. Laughing is an important part of celebration but I felt a sadness that our front-end formative work was over.

Tuesday 28 September 1993

A dark morning and it feels like winter. Yesterday was worse — the coldest day in September for 42 years! But it does seem to have warmed up today a bit. I'm working in the office first of all, then going to Kensington for lunch with a client.

Thursday 30 September 1993

Yesterday Helen had presented to the management team a set of recommendations. But all the UK management team are leaving the company, rather than moving to Holland, and would not commit to anything. Helen was frustrated and disappointed.

It was an important day for Helen as she had put in her application for voluntary severance. Her job has also moved to the Holland office. Applying now, she may or may not be granted severance pay. If she is, she will receive a lump sum now and a small annual income from the age of 50. Helen sees this as an opportunity to take some new, as yet unspecified, direction.

Wednesday 6 October 1993

Farnborough. A strategy awayday with a hotel client and his direct reports. They need to put together a strategic plan for a group of 12 hotels. Straightforward stuff . We started with a team roles exercise, then turned to the business and defined objectives, issues and information needs.

PROJECT PLAN

CLIENT: HOTEL COMPANY B

	SEPT	OCT	NOV	DEC	JAN
1. BRIEFING					
2. FACILITATE STRATEGY AWAY DAYS					
3. SUPPORT MANAGERS IN PRODUCING STRATEGIC PLANS					

STRATEGIC DEVELOPMENT PROJECT

Halfway through the afternoon, the group was moving slowly through some difficult terrain. A participant asked me why I was so serious and not involved in all the banter. I suppose I was focused on making progress in the meeting. It made me reflect on what a facilitator does: could I properly do my job and have a laugh at the same time? No, I would become drawn in. With hindsight the facilitator should have called 'time out' before this point, and indicated to the group that they were getting stuck.

Value through calling time out

I was reluctant to stop the group when the going got tough, but I realized afterwards that I would add more value by stopping the group to review progress than by letting them struggle on.

EMPLOYEES

CUSTOMERS

SHAREHOLDERS

BALANCING NEEDS AND INTERESTS

Thursday 14 October 1993

Three client meetings. The first was at 8am with a local authority client. Office was above a borough library. Good meeting, leaving me free to develop a programme and materials for next week's facilitation skills course.

Met second client in hotel near Heathrow. Presented a paper on 'congruent objectives': the three main people constituencies in any business (employees, customers and shareholders) are a sort of golden triangle to be held in balance. Each has a current size and a larger potential size. Provided the needs and interests of each group are honoured then the company can grow. This hotel company has limited its growth to date by focusing short-term on the shareholder neglecting customer and employee. Client listened carefully and agreed.

Third meeting was with healthcare client who questioned me about how I keep in touch with leading-edge people and ideas. I told him about professional groups and conferences I go to. We talked about networking. He said if I made him a proposal ('I really want to do this') and showed enough enthusiasm, his reaction would always be 'yes'.

He went on to propose three new projects: an R&D project into 'life-changing' development for trainers, a presentation on measuring education and a re-fit of the course Joe and I developed. Busy again! The third good meeting. A good day.

Value through meeting clients
Face-to-face client contact led to further project work in all three cases.

Value through developing a model
The model helped the client to put into words something that he wanted to express about 'congruent objectives'. I

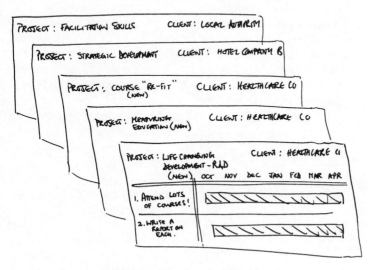

FURTHER PROJECT WORK

also felt satisfied to be able to express something that had been troubling me over the last seven years with this client: the exploitation of staff and the neglect of customers. The model provided an acceptable way to do this.

Value through feedback from the client

I learned that, to Richard, I came across as serious, professional perhaps, but lacking in visible positive energy and more keen to be right than anything else.

Sunday 17 October 1993

The weather has turned from very wet to very cold. We woke up today to a hard frost, and the lawn was white.

Monday 18 October 1993

It was a long time since we had spoken, and Joe had a lot to say. He had discovered some dangerous 'blindspots' in the change programme.

The first blindspot was 'managing change' and 'stress'. What was the organization doing to raise its knowledge and skills in this area? Not much. Any change programme involves setting 'stretch goals'. Every 'stretch goal' is a 'stress goal'. Facilitators and trainers were taking on an extra 50% workload on top of their day jobs, but stress management has not been on the agenda. There is a macho view of change: set tough objectives, use charisma and vision to inspire people.

The second blindspot was 'not training middle managers' who are the 'process owners'. The top 500 or so people, the 'process sponsors', went through leadership training but still haven't learnt either to manage change and/or to select processes and projects for improvement. Facilitators are well trained

PROJECT PLAN	1993 JAN	F	M	A	M	J	J	A	S	O	N	D	1994 J
1.TOP 300 MANAGERS	▨												
2.TRAINING 50,000 STAFF				DESIGN	DELIVER								
3.CEO RETIRES													✳

CLIENT: HEALTHCARE CO.

NEW MEGA PROJECT

but very junior in the hierarchy relative to the process owners and sponsors. This limits their ability to train and influence process owners. How does it feel to be a process owner? Not good. How prepared are process owners to get involved in improvement projects? Not at all.

The third blindspot is 'project management'. This is the biggest competence gap. A self-study module was produced but it became bogged down in politics and was not issued.

In summary, he seemed quite downhearted. It was a mixed picture: initial trainer/facilitator training was good; readiness and planning good in places but patchy; leader training poor and incomplete; top-level leadership of the change programme ambiguous; quality of facilitator training sacrificed in pursuit of numbers trained; too many starter projects being initiated; most trainers inexperienced in facilitation; further education needs not addressed.

ITEM	RESULT
INITIAL TRAINING	✓
READINESS / PLANNING	MIXED
LEADER TRAINING	POOR, INCOMPLETE
TOP LEVEL LEADERSHIP	AMBIGUOUS
NUMBERS TRAINED	✓
QUALITY OF CANDIDATES	MIXED
STARTER PROJECTS	TOO MANY
EXPERIENCE OF DOING FACILITATION	LOW
FURTHER EDUCATION NEEDS	NOT ADDRESSED

BLINDSPOTS

Value through noticing the client's tone of voice

The client needed to express all this but still seemed stuck afterwards. I was confused about what to do. I now realize it was up to me to highlight to the client the sad and resigned tone of his voice – and then to see how he wanted to take things forward.

Value through confronting the underlying issue

I felt that the client had anticipated these problems ahead of time, but no one would listen to him. The issue was not whether his analysis was right. I had no doubt of this. The real issue was why they didn't listen. I did not realize this at the time.

Tuesday 19 October 1993

Helen saw me from her taxi as she was returning from the airport. I was walking down our road to pick up the kids. She said I was a slumped, listless, grey figure. This is how I felt too — a little tired, flogging myself to work hard and feeling little reward from it.

Value through gaining feedback

Until Helen commented on my appearance I had little idea that I was looking tired. This made me think about my work pace and my ability to add value if my batteries are run down.

Monday 25 October 1993

Glossy staff magazine lying in reception with 'Education and Training' headline. I opened it eagerly to find a section headed 'Now we're doing the training'. Below there were photos of trainers with quotes beneath about their experiences of training:

> The five day course was one of the most challenging I've ever had or taught. The feedback I hear is 'how great it is to see our own people training us'.

> I liked the way the workshops approached facilitation with a real-life focus: What are the key things a facilitator needs to know? Where are the pitfalls?

> I have done things I had no idea I could do, and to be able to train and develop others in new ways of working is tremendously exciting as well as personally rewarding.

> In the workshops if someone did something clever (or embarrassing) everyone would laugh and give a round of applause. I'm still amazed at the friendships, enthusiasm and support being carried forward. To this day I can pick up the phone and call any of the people I trained with.

I liked what I read but, when I reflected on it, I found it incomplete. The glossy magazine was upbeat as staff communications so often are. Its tone reflected my feelings about the change programme as they were around June/July. But the concerns that Joe had recently expressed as blindspots were the real issues now. The magazine seems dishonest in not referring to these issues directly.

OK, it takes time to produce a glossy magazine, but one of my first questions as a consumer of the printed word is 'Is this trustworthy?'. I am not alone in this. This magazine, perhaps through its delay or otherwise, through its editorial policy (good news only), fails the test. It was a smokescreen disguising the truth.

FIGHT BACK

REFLECTIONS

Reflections on the fight back phase

What was really going on?

When I committed to working with the healthcare company, I did this without reference to my existing commitments to family and other clients. In fact, fearing a shortage of work later, and on top of the already stretching healthcare assignment, I took on even more work with other clients. I ended up short-changing Helen, the kids and some of my clients. There was not much joy in life at this time. The job was exciting in many respects but, looking at life in a wider sense, it was a dull grind.

What is my theory about why?

I needed to recover from 'Fall' in the previous phase, and I did not want to let anyone see me being hurt by my mistake with Edward. It was a matter of pride or self-esteem.

I felt strong enough to cope. I did not realize where my limits were. Once I had contracted to doing a project, I became very fixed and committed to delivering it. During this phase I was busier and I was earning more than in years. By the end I had more forward bookings than ever before. With hindsight, my frenetic work in this phase seems to be an overreaction to my fear of failure in the previous phase.

Feedback from Richard and Helen had forced me to notice that I was not looking good; I was overloaded with work worries and far too serious. I had not forgotten what I learnt the previous year about being authentic, but I had temporarily stopped growing in that direction and had probably slipped back. I was a mass of contra-dictions.

I had compromised some of my values in taking on the healthcare assignment. I was unable to influence the programme to my satisfaction, partly through joining it too late. I felt frustrated. My ultimatum over payment was an expression of both this frustration and my powerlessness in the other areas of the assignment.

EXERCISE: LOCATING VALUE

The author's journey was fuelled by his search for
ever higher value in the client relationship.
Consider the value you are creating through your
client relationships.

EXERCISE

1 **Think of a recent meeting with a client. Reflect
   on both facts and the feelings involved. Write a
   brief summary of the meeting.**

2 **What value (intended and unintended) did you
   gain from the meeting?**

3 **What value did the client gain from the
   meeting?**

How do you know?

4 **What did you both do that helped to create this value?**

5 **Review the value commentaries in this book so far. List some new or different possibilities you can now see for creating value with your client.**

Phase 3: Explore

EXPLORE

The third phase of the journey was an exploration of new experiences, new awareness and new ways of working. There were a number of development courses. A report was written on 'Life Changing Development'. The work content shifted to incorporate interpersonal feedback, coaching and new approaches to facilitation.

Tuesday 9 November 1993

The barber cut the mole on my neck with a cut-throat razor, then applied a styptic pencil to stop the bleeding. I was quiet at the time: he apologized and treated this as routine. The pencil caused an unpleasant stinging which I could bear – I knew it would soon pass.

It was just an uncomfortable feeling – a disquiet at first. The barber cut me. It hurt. Then he used the pencil to stop the bleeding. That hurt more. Then there is AIDs. Was the pencil disposable? No. Was it sterilized? I don't think so. Why are they not aware of the risk? Are they? Am I? No, I was just afraid.

Value through not harming the client
I know that a facilitator, a consultant or a coach can hurt people. We can harm their feelings easily. They can feel a risk or a threat in the things we say and do. To them, we can seem out of control, like the barber with the cut-throat razor. The client can feel vulnerable just as I did in the barber's shop. The emotions experienced are probably similar. Pain. Outrage. Righteous anger. A desire to right the wrong.

TRUSTING THE PILOT

Wednesday 10 November 1993

Georgia and I watched a video we made of my balloon ride. We met the balloon pilot in a park in Skipton one summer evening. The ride took me over Pendle Hill into Lancashire. We landed with a bump in a field beside the Clitheroe bypass, having avoided two previous fields, one with a fierce-looking bull and another with an electricity pylon. The ride was a thrill. I had total confidence in the pilot – my life was in his hands.

Value through trusting
I realized that my trust in the pilot was implicit. It arose from a range of factors including Helen's confidence to make the booking, the look of the equipment, the ease with which the pilot unpacked the balloon and inflated it,

his small actions and his facial expression. There was nothing at all that cast doubt on his ability. It is difficult for any facilitator or consultant to be so self-assured. Our task is more complex. If we are not sure of our methods then how can we expect our clients to put their lives in our hands?

Wednesday 17 November 1993

The client was in a good mood. In our project we had reached the top of the mountain. We chatted over lunch about healthcare trivia. Pumpkin seeds are used in Germany to ease pain from prostate conditions. Badedas bath oil has horse chestnut extract as the active ingredient but it is not declared to avoid possible pressures to class Badedas as a medicine. He has the most amazing memory for information.

Our conversation turned to self-administered diagnostic products that put people in charge of their own bodies – of their own healthcare instead of this being a poorly administered state responsibility through the health service. We talked of developing an expert system, harnessing the knowledge of clinicians, allowing clinicians to move to a higher value-added role. We noted that resistance of the medical establishment to change could be a significant barrier.

Value through finding a motivating subject

Discussing the healthcare breakthrough project was uplifting for both of us. This conversation was light-hearted. We were not trying to create value for the company. The subject seemed to grip us. It connected with a deeper motivation. We became immersed in it. It felt creative and special.

Thursday 18 November 1993

I awoke happy, glowing. The frost was thick, the sky was clear and sunny. I reflected on the ups and downs of life. I seem to be getting more of them, or perhaps I am just more aware of them. This week, in the space of two days, my mood has swung from the blackest depths up into my current carefree state, drifting along on the clouds.

Evening outing to Nursery Curriculum evening which was a slide show by teacher in the school hall on what they teach in nursery. Mrs Leonard, the teacher, did a wonderful job communicating the magic of the nursery, starting and ending with a reading. The closing reading was by Robert Fulghum. I found this very moving.

> Most of what I really need to know about how to live, and what to do and how to be, I learned in kindergarten. Wisdom was not at the top of the graduate school mountain but there in the sandbox, at nursery school.
>
> These are the things I learned: share everything. Play fair. Don't hit people. Put things back where you found them. Clean up your own mess. Don't take things that aren't yours. Say you're sorry when you hurt somebody. Wash your hands before you eat. Flush. Warm cookies and cold milk are good for you. Live a balanced life. Learn some, think some and draw and paint and sing and dance and play every day some. Take a nap every afternoon.
>
> When you go into the world watch for traffic, hold hands and stick together. Be aware of wonder. Remember the little seed in the plastic cup. The roots go down and the plant goes up and nobody really knows how or why, but we are all like that. Goldfish and hamsters and white mice and even the little seed in the plastic cup — they all die. So do we.
>
> And then remember the book about Dick and Jane and the first word you learned, the biggest word of all: LOOK.
>
> Everything you need to know is in there somewhere: the golden rule and love and basic sanitation, ecology and politics and sane living.
>
> Think of what a better world it would be if we all — the whole world — had cookies and milk about 3 o'clock

every afternoon and then lay down with our blankets for a nap. Or if we had a basic policy in our nation, and in other nations, to always put things back where we found them and to clean up our own messes. And it is still true, no matter how old you are, when you go out into the world, it is best to hold hands and stick together.

Sunday 21 November 1993

We awoke to snow. The kids were very excited. Georgia does not remember snow. She was just a tiny baby last time. It is three years since Tom has seen any. They both came to the newsagents with me, happy as larks making snowballs and footprints. They came back and played in the garden while I read the paper. Tom made a snowman.

Tuesday 23 November 1993

I started the day by writing a reliable 'method for facilitating a meeting' which captured much of the experience I have gained as a facilitator over the years. When I had finished, it seemed both an important and obvious thing to want to do, yet it had never previously occurred to me.

I set off at 6pm for the Gatwick hotel with flipcharts and materials in the boot, ready to do a really good job.

Lovely hotel, comfortable room, VIP bottle of wine waiting on ice in the room. My brief tonight was to run a brainstorming session on 'the hotel product in the year 2001' after a dinner in the hotel's Chinese restaurant. We brainstormed until 11.30pm, way past my bedtime, and produced over 150 ideas, some of them very good.

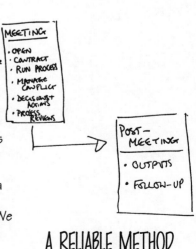

A RELIABLE METHOD

Value through flexibility

Client gained value from my flexibility – working in the restaurant and working late.

Value through brainstorming

Amazing success at producing ideas in volume, thinking 'outside the box'. We all became tired though. Some participants became a little worried about what to do with all the ideas. Next time I'll explain the process more carefully so that people understand how the ideas are captured, sorted and used.

Wednesday 24 November 1993

Workshop continued at Gatwick. Good meeting. We sifted the 150 ideas from last night into categories. We reviewed progress on the business plan: there was confusion about the format. We spent some time on this and pennies started to drop. We developed a Statement of Intent. This took longer than expected – two hours instead of one – but we revamped the timetable, extended the finish time and recovered quite well.

I built in some real participation and learning to the meeting. I gave out team performance rating scales and called a Process Review (what is working well?/what isn't?) at lunchtime and at the end. I learned from this that one participant had been really bothered by our earlier difficulties about the business plan format. He felt others were not taking responsibility and that the meeting was losing direction.

By contrast, others seemed to respond positively to the opportunity to discuss the meeting itself in the Process Review. They were gaining control.

STRATEGIC
DEVELOPMENT PROJECT

The Process Reviews put me on a much firmer footing as the facilitator – well informed and in control. I was able to ask for, and listen to, comments using the objective background of the team rating scales and the what worked?/what didn't? format.

After the meeting I felt recharged as a facilitator. I felt good, decisive, vindicated in the time taken yesterday to write the reliable method for facilitation. I was asked to facilitate another meeting in December and to continue supporting the team in developing their business plan.

PROCESS REVIEWS

Value through encouraging client learning

The client expected me to operate as I used to – taking firm control of the meeting, being highly directive and task-driven, tightly controlling the time. Sometimes you make more progress when you let go of control and trust the client. There are two styles of facilitation: task-centred and learning-centred. When effectively done, the first creates a dependency on the facilitator and allows participants to slip into a childlike passivity waiting for parental guidance (from the facilitator). The second mode requires participants to take greater responsibility and generates more learning. Today's meeting was an early experiment with the second method.

Value through defining a reliable method

The experiment arose from yesterday's overdue exercise of defining a reliable method for facilitating a meeting. This had enabled me to encapsulate many accumulated lessons and put my learning into practice.

Thursday 25 November 1993

Course on Accelerated Learning about using the whole brain, engaging all the senses to speed up learning. It was most interesting. I felt inspired to make the training environment more 'impactful' using more of the following:

PROJECT: LIFE CHANGING DEVELOPMENT – RAD   CLIENT: HEALTHCARE COMPANY

	OCT	NOV	DEC	JAN	FEB	MAR	APR
1. BRIEFING	▌						
2. ACCELERATED LEARNING COURSE		▌					

- icebreakers
- pictures
- sound: music
- colour
- creating a relaxing environment for right-brain learning
- participants inventing solutions for themselves even with complex matters such as health and safety, manufacturing logistics, financial statements.

LIFE CHANGING DEVELOPMENT PROJECT

Saturday 27 November 1993

Went on our bikes to Hampton Court to watch a medieval battle. Enquiries revealed that people in medieval dress were in the King's Arms public house. When we got inside it was warm, exciting but a bit frightening for Tom and Georgia – people dressed up in helmets and carrying swords were coming up to them, asking questions.

Tom tested a 'medieval fruit machine' in which three ladies in full period dress held a bag containing pieces of real fruit. After the shout of 'pull!' from Tom, each pulled out one piece. If, for example, all three pulled out apples, then the player wins, just like a one-armed bandit. A local newspaper photographer took Tom's picture.

Value through remembering the human dimension

This low-tech 'medieval' game encompassed many important human and social elements that we seem to forget in modern life. It invited involvement, participation without demanding any particular knowledge, skill or intelligence. It was fun for all: the three ladies, the gamblers and the audience. Age did not matter. We were united in a common entertainment.

Compare this to the modern fruit machine: a solitary person stands hypnotized in the corner in front of the sound and flashing lights, pushing in more and more money. The machine is an annoying distraction to others in the bar.

The first game involves love. In the rush to high-tech, silicon-based, multimedia solutions we can easily miss the important human dimension.

Tuesday 30 November 1993

Afternoon meeting with Barry. I last visited his house ten months ago and learned some interesting things about the future shape of the consulting industry.

The meeting today was to vet me for Barry's course. It lasted one and a half hours. Barry seemed experienced and wise, but was less dominant than I expected. He allowed me to make much of the running. I told him quite a lot. I was able to be quite open.

What did I learn?

- I am more aware than most consultants of the client relationship: yet I still feel this is a shortcoming.
- There is an old school in consulting where the emphasis is more on expertise than relationship or process. This operates as an age factor. My old consulting firm was mostly old-school.
- I have already made great progress in my practice, building stronger client relationships and using the diary as a learning tool.
- I am interested in making Page Consulting

PROJECT: LIFE CHANGING DEVELOPMENT – R&D		CLIENT: HEALTHCARE COMPANY					
	OCT	NOV	DEC	JAN	FEB	MAR	APR
1. BRIEFING	▨						
2. ACCELERATED LEARNING COURSE		▨					
3. MARESFIELD CURNOW COURSE			▨				
4. AMED TRANS. DEVELOPMENT				▨			

LIFE CHANGING
DEVELOPMENT PROJECT

self-renewing and distinctive, where learning is part of the normal operating practice.
- Barry sees me as occupying the same niche as the Alexander Corporation, The Coaching House, The Results Partnership . . . and yet I see me as different.
- The healthcare company story is a good one: I could benefit from talking more about it. The implementation know-how I have is valuable.
- There is enough work for everyone in this business. It is up to me to be distinctive, then I do not have to compete directly with others.

I am looking forward to the programme. Each module includes tutorials to help me make the connections I need. I valued the depth of exposure Barry has in the consulting industry and I felt that, as my mentor, I could learn a lot from him.

Value through encouraging the client to talk

Barry's questioning left me doing most of the talking. Only occasionally would he join in to interpret or add his perspective. I felt that I was making sense of my diverse and confused professional experience with someone who understood what I was talking about. This was satisfying and valuable.

Tuesday 14 December 1993

AMED (Association of Management Education and Development) course called Transformational Development. Valuable.

Judy Rosener in 'Ways Women Lead' said that women leaders motivate others to transform their goals into the goals of the organization. How? By:

1 encouraging participation
2 sharing power and information
3 enhancing others' self-worth
4 energizing others through their own enthusiasm.

Men, on the other hand, are dumbheads who think they can lead using formal structure/position, rewards and punishments as their tools.

That's the theory, but it was the experience that was most valuable. It started with 30 or so people sitting in a large circle with three female presenters at the front. One of them spoke about male/female stereotypes and I noticed there were about five males against 30 or so females. There was discussion. I felt uncomfortable: I was a minority, without a voice, the villain, talked over, talked past, isolated. It all got sticky, with attempts to redefine and bridge differences. We ended up failing and blaming 'the inadequacy of language'.

Around 11.30 I had not learned anything, and the pace was too slow. Shortly afterwards it was lunchtime and I realized we were almost there. I remember someone talking later on, over lunch, about how sometimes 'time becomes elastic' when facilitating and I felt I knew exactly what she meant.

After the stuck point, pairs developed ground rules for the day. We introduced one another (self, work role, what you value about people). This involved us, encouraged gentle self-disclosure. My self-worth was creeping back up. I felt included again. Safety/trust levels in the group became high. I was receptive to a presentation that followed: a story about how a women's group got started. Then more about male/female differences. Self-interest had been transformed in the 'here and now': we were a cohesive group.

Trios continued in discussion over lunch. I realized how low self-worth produces closure, insecurity, argumentative defensiveness, stuckness and is a barrier to change. I discovered concerns about the healthcare company change programme:

- Is self-interest really being transformed into corporate?
- If the leaders or trainers answered 'yes', then would facilitators, middle managers or 52,000 staff worldwide agree with them?

TRANSFORMING DIFFERENCES

Some exercises promote self-interest (e.g. male vs. female) producing separateness, undermining collective strength. Others build understanding and inclusion. Awareness of this point is a most important underpinning to facilitation skill.

Value through transforming self-interest into corporate

This session taught me some principles for combining individuals' energies in teams and in corporations. Permitting the individual to exist fully, as themselves, warts and all, enables them to open up, engage with and offer their energies to others. By contrast, we see corporations generally restricting individuals, imposing upon them and controlling them more like slaves. Individuals then close down and play a narrow, political and low-energy game.

Value through 'here and now' learning

Once I surrendered to the process and became fully involved, I began to learn at a deeper level. I learnt through my feelings – through my heart – not just through my thinking. This 'here and now' learning was more powerful at the time; it was faster and has proved more enduring.

STRATEGIC DEVELOPMENT PROJECT

Thursday 16 December 1993

Final meeting at Heathrow hotel – facilitating the team that is putting together a business plan. At the start they were apologizing, disappointed and embarrassed at their lack of progress. There was an air of resignation, impossibility, giving up.

   I did a very simple facilitation job: I got each individual to take stock of their actual progress, then I recorded their concerns and questioned them so they could evolve their action plan.

   At the end, they reported feeling better; they knew what to do and they could now deliver the plan within the set deadline.

Value through enquiring, listening and watching
The team had given up. The most effective facilitation can be very simple. It usually starts with enquiring, listening and watching. In this case the value was enormous because the group's energy level was transformed.

TRANSFORMING THE GROUP'S ENERGY

Friday 31 December 1993

New Year's Eve. I was sent out at midnight with a lump of coal, a piece of bread and a silver coin to knock on the door and bring good luck. The man over the road was out too, doing the same thing!

Monday 3 January 1994

My two themes for 1994 will be 'simplify' and 'stretch'. The first is relatively easy: simpler admin. and performance measures. The second is still a puzzle that I am hoping to unravel. Any stretch must begin where we are now, from known strengths and established values. I am not ready to make any leaps in the dark. I want to define a clear, attractive path for the business.

Value through annual business planning

Planning is a step in the learning loop: plan, do, review. My annual plan begins with a review of last year: highs and lows. Then I ask myself what I want to create or accomplish over the coming period. By planning at the start of the year, I put in place a set of support arrangements for the work. This frees me from distractions so that, for most of my working time, I can be dedicated to creating value with clients.

Sunday 9 January 1994

EXPRESSION

* The new challenge

SELF-ESTEEM — ✓ Mostly Satisfied

SECURITY — ? Occasional threats to security

SURVIVAL — ✓ Mostly Satisfied

MASLOW'S HIERARCHY

After our swim we all stepped on to the scales. I have put on three stone since Helen and I first met 15 years ago. Last year I became less active and my weight increased by almost a stone. I have started going to the gym and swimming, hoping to find a new equilibrium.

Helen and I discussed where we wanted to get to in 12 months' time. We got a bit stuck. I wanted the roof replaced. We seem to want to maintain, rather than transform, our lives.

We talked about what it is like to reach the 'self-actualizing' point above the survival, financial and self-esteem needs in Maslow's hierarchy. You express yourself fully through some central life activity. It becomes a total expression of yourself: who you are, what you have done so far and what you are uniquely qualified to do.

Monday 18 January 1994

Barry's course in Hampstead. I listed some principles I would wish to be present in every relationship. We talked about what transforming a relationship really means, what 'life-changing' means and where I recognize barriers and risks in developing others.

The tutor used his non-directive counselling skills to help me define some principles to steer through a minefield of development approaches (such as counselling, coaching, mentoring, NLP, Gestalt, co-counselling etc.).

We explored the problems of cults (such as the Moonies), the conversion and deconversion process, evangelism and quasi-religious forms of development. I learned that development activities that are corporately sponsored must be voluntary, confidential and free of peer pressure. Otherwise they become divisive, confusing, damaging and immoral.

In counselling, people will only go as far as they want to in revealing deep-seated feelings. If counselling takes place in a public setting where peers are able to observe, a person might feel afterwards that they have been raped or violated. Informed consent is needed. If people feel long-term regret about it, then that experience can be taken to have been damaging.

Value through creating the conditions for conversation

The tutor had succeeded in creating a set of conditions in which I was able to explore these questions which were deep and difficult for me.

Tuesday 19 January 1994

I watched a TV programme about teenagers and their parents talking about sex. John Heron, a leading psychologist/facilitator, previously at the University of Surrey, was helping people act out the situation, to replay incomplete and blocked situations, to bring up

PROJECT: LIFE CHANGING DEVELOPMENT – R&D		CLIENT: HEALTHCARE COMPANY					
	OCT	NOV	DEC	JAN	FEB	MAR	APR
1. BRIEFING	▨						
2. ACCELERATED LEARNING COURSE		▨					
3. MARLESFIELD CURNOW COURSE			▨		▨		
4. AMED TRANS. DEVELOPMENT			▮				
5. AMED – CLIENT RELATIONSHIPS				▮			

LIFE CHANGING DEVELOPMENT PROJECT

their feelings around those situations and to learn.

His input was minimal; he provided a safe environment, invited people to participate, maintained a relationship of trust with all, stopped things to review and brought in helpers to provide support through just standing nearby or touching the shoulders of participants. He was very low-key but effective through encouraging trust. Helen and I were surprised at the willingness of people to play, including a teenage boy who had to ask his dad in the middle of a simulated burger bar, whether he masturbated.

Thursday 20 January 1994

Attended AMED course at Covent Garden on Managing Client Relationships. The learning point I took away was about one's credentials and legitimacy as a provider of certain services. Cross-selling is encouraged within every large consulting firm, but what are the limits of the

CREDENTIALS

salesperson's credibility? The answer was put across clearly and forcibly with the tutor's challenge: 'Would you buy central heating from your solicitor?'

Value through credentials
I relearned about how a promise must be supported by credentials. The client is placing trust in you just as you do with an aeroplane pilot.

Sunday 23 January 1994

Helen and I watched a video called Groundhog Day about a weatherman who relives one day time and again until he transforms from a narrow selfish one-dimensional being into a balanced, educated and fulfilled person who then marries the leading lady, Andie McDowell. This seems to strongly support a theme of self-development, learning, personal growth and change.

Thursday 27 January 1994

Five years ago, the healthcare company client had selected an approach to managing change designed by Warner Burke and George Litwin. It had been tested by applied research in BA, Exxon and NASA. It consists of 12 boxes (plus feedback loops connecting them) labelled:

External Environment, Leadership, Mission/Strategy, Culture, Management Practices, Structure, Systems, Work Unit Climate, Tasks/Abilities, Motivation, Individual Needs/Values, Performance.

Over the last five years the company's management committee had systematically tackled each box.

Value through a special style of conversation

We have all noticed programmes that disappoint or fail because they do not reach right to the heart of the change issues in a company. I am uncomfortable that the 12-box model enabled 'talking about change' without reaching the central issues. The style of the conversation seems to be the key. I have recently noticed special conversations that engage participants at a deeply personal level, touching their hearts not just their heads. This is the style needed to get real insight, movement and change. Special conversations need to take place right through the business hierarchy, not just at the top.

Saturday 29 January 1994

Awoke in the villa at Center Parcs in Sherwood Forest, Nottingham. Jogged to the shop for a newspaper and some eggs. We spent most of the day swimming in the 'sub-tropical paradise'.

Value through relaxation and exercise

They say a healthy body creates a healthy mind. Exercise does actually lift my mood.

Thursday 3 February 1994

Di, my client in Australia in 1992, visited us. She had been in the UK for a course on facilitation skills. Helen and I took her out for dinner at Le Petit Max. I learned some very positive facts about the longer-term results of our work. I also gained updates on a couple of problem people.

Value through speaking truth

My conversation with Di was one in which the client was able to unfold their version of the truth without worrying about how it looked or sounded: in other words, without worrying about image or politics. Most conversations in the competitive and insecure world of business are not like this. Truth is blocked.

I am finding that only in conversations where real truth is expressed is there a real potential for change. No wonder change is difficult in business!

Monday 14 February 1994

The fourth module in Barry's course. The question of how to build relationships and organizations strongly was looming large in my mind. This must be at the core of what I wish to offer. The consulting and facilitation skills I use and teach are the ones that help achieve this.

Value through noticing what you have in mind

The theme of building organizations strongly has been implicit and invisible until this point. Yet in this area I feel a strong motivation which is a clue to where I can create the greatest value with my clients. I needed the special reflective kind of environment provided here to be able to notice this.

Tuesday 15 February 1994

PROJECT PLAN 1994 FEB

CLIENT: COMPUTER SUPPORT CONSULTANT

1. INITIAL COACHING SESSION
2. ??

COACHING PROJECT

I did some free consulting with a self-employed computer support person who had been 'stuck in a quagmire' since Christmas. The session took place at his home/office. Before it I faxed him a list of the mistakes and setbacks I had faced in business over the last six years.

We started with some 'contracting' around what the session was for and 'ground rules' to make it effective. Then I asked him to list 20 'achievements' (self-esteem building), 20 'incompletions', 20 'threats/risks' he faces followed by action planning and a review.

I made notes in Mind Map form to capture the key points he made, enabling me to summarize easily. After the review he wanted to make his plan more specific and we looked at his weekly time use (current and desired).

What did I learn? That being open with him about my six years of mistakes encouraged him to be honest with me. That he recognizes some of his own faults, such as getting away with cheating on time etc. That he needed a plan at the end of the session that was achievable and realistic. To be flexible myself and stay in communication with the client through reviews (for example, I stayed to firm up the action plan in response to one of his expressed concerns).

At the end, the situation already feels less desperate. The client seems confident he will solve his problem.

Value through noticing a shift in the client's energy

I felt a change in the client's energy: at the beginning he was mired in failure; during the session he was stepping outside and exploring his situation; by the end he wanted to move ahead with an achievable action plan.

SHARING MY MISTAKES · GROUNDRULES

FINDING THE CLIENT'S ENERGY

STAY FLEXIBLE · 20 ACHIEVEMENTS

ACTION PLAN · 20 RISKS/THREATS · 20 INCOMPLETIONS

USING MIND MAPS

Thursday 17 February 1994

Yet another course, called 'Transitions in Consulting'. The atmosphere (as at all AMED events) was quite warm and supportive, encouraging me to be authentic.

Four of us were discussing together in a subgroup 'how to create a secure base for our consulting work'. We decided to look 'inside ourselves' for the answers rather than outside at the team or organization context. After about 20 minutes it was time to stop but I didn't want to: I was immersed in the discussion. The feeling in our group was mutual.

What was so special? We were sharing and giving each other time to contribute. We were building on each others' experience. We were disclosing confidences. I spoke about the relationship principles I had been working on. Two others were into NLP and showed us how they express their fundamental values and beliefs through feelings and pictures rather than words. Someone else spoke of wanting to get out of the corporation, and about using 'clowning' as a means of expressing his feelings.

We were given a little extra time to finish. At the end of this, when it was time to report in plenary, one of the others said 'Look at the four of them – they're blissed out'.

'Blissed out' is the valuable learning for me from this event. It is the feeling of relaxed contentment I have when I have shared confidences with another person in an equal way, where the only goal is learning for the two individuals. 'Blissed out' is a powerful feeling. I felt at my best. I felt included, accepted and understood. I felt great.

Value through sharing deep personal insights

This was a valuable experience of a special environment in which people can share deep personal insights. It is still memorable. An immediate effect was a new interest in using feelings and pictures, rather than words, to express my deeper purpose and values. When I look at my later writings on Flow Theory and generativity, I recognize that this 'blissed out' experience was the seed.

Friday 18 February 1994

PROJECT:	LIFE CHANGING DEVELOPMENT - R&D			CLIENT: HEALTHCARE COMPANY			
	OCT	NOV	DEC	JAN	FEB	MAR	APR
1. BRIEFING	▨						
2. ACCELERATED LEARNING COURSE		▨					
3. MARESFIELD CURNOW COURSE			▨		▨	▨	
4. AMED TRANS. DEVELOPMENT				▨			
5. AMED - CLIENT RELATIONSHIPS				▨			
6. AMED - TRANSITIONS					▨		
7. WRITE & PRESENT REPORT				▨▨▨▨			

LIFE CHANGING DEVELOPMENT PROJECT

The client had read my 'Life Changing Development' report and said he appreciated it, but he seemed more interested in what I myself was gaining from all my recent development activity. Later, when his assistant popped in, they exchanged a few words. She asked me how I was, how work was going. I said 'fine'. The client said 'Look at him!'. She said, yes, I was different, it showed on my face, I was enjoying myself.

I felt slightly uneasy being talked about, but I did realize how serious and burdened I must have seemed to them over the last 11 months. I was pleased they cared; they seemed interested in the quality of my experience.

Then she left, and the client went on to disclose a great deal about himself. He told me of his personal mission statement, his vision of his future and his ambitions. He told me about a Lou Tice development programme.

Value through quality of contact

This meeting was exceptional. There was a quality of contact. I suppose we were relating as people, thinking about ourselves and each other for a change instead of the company.

Tuesday 1 March 1994

A day in the office using a process mapping method to simplify our admin. Identified seven core processes we need to manage in order to deliver long-term value to clients:

- marketing/PR
- handling enquiries
- doing projects
- follow-up
- servicing clients
- admin. and management
- learning/development/ strategy/ improvement.

I need to spread my time across these activities. If, for example, I spend enough time on follow-up/servicing, this will generate new work opportunities from the existing client base.

INPUT   PROCESS   OUTPUTS

1. MARKETING | PR
2. CLIENT SERVICE
TIME 3. HANDLING → 4. DOING → 5. FOLLOW-UP   • MONEY
        ENQUIRIES   PROJECTS   MEETINGS   • QUALITY
6. BUSINESS ADMIN. AND MANAGEMENT   OF WORK
7. LEARNING: STRATEGY, IMPROVEMENT   AND LIFE

SEVEN CORE PROCESSES IN A CONSULTANCY BUSINESS

Value through defining simple performance measures

Through doing this process mapping, I belatedly realized that time use is one of my key measures: a way of ensuring that I achieve the right business outputs (money, quality of work, good client relationships, quality of life and so on).

Wednesday 2 March 1994

I drove to the client meeting, listening to a Lou Tice personal development tape. I am halfway through. His ideas are delivered in a slow, ambling, reassuring and anecdotal style. This style puts some people off, but I am finding his ideas about learning, comfort zones, vision, affirmations, self-talk and so on quite compelling. It gives you a framework from which you can take care of your own personal development.

Your mind works creatively and unconsciously to bring about change. All you need to do is clarify your personal vision (V) and notice, in contrast, what current reality (CR) is like. Your 'creative unconscious', like a quiet and faithful servant, will do the rest for you.

This framework helps me to explain changes and the unfolding of events in my life to date. It helps me to relax.

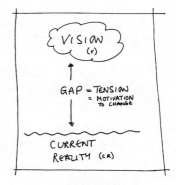

VISION (V)

GAP = TENSION = MOTIVATION TO CHANGE

CURRENT REALITY (CR)

PERSONAL DEVELOPMENT METHOD

When we focus clearly on an intention, in due course it unfolds and happens for us. I need not be so driven, provided I do a little reflective work to get clear on my true intentions. We can 'programme' ourselves to gain and become more the person we wish to be.

Value through being mentally stimulated
Listening to the tapes was like certain good conversations: I could feel the synapses firing, connections being made, new possibilities emerging.

Thursday 3 March 1994

Rob and I are due to work together on a 'measurement of education' project, and this was our first meeting.

He disclosed much of his implicit agenda, and I felt I was able to reveal a little of my own. Rob is very concerned with the theories of Deming, the promotion of McGregor's Theory Y (as opposed to Theory X) and with increasing the understanding of statistical methods in the company at large.

Trust grows from this kind of disclosure. We did a brief, two-minute review at the end. We noticed that we were listening well to one another and were off to a good start. We both want to get going. It was a good meeting.

Value through sharing hidden agendas
I felt a quality and a genuineness in our discussion. If we had not created the conditions to reach to the hidden agendas I think our discussion would have been shallow and formal and our working relationship fragile.

Tuesday 8 March 1994

I have a personal vision of 'a mutually supporting network of relationships'. I used to feel as though I was ploughing a lonely furrow, unnoticed and unsupported. Only recently conceived, there are signs of the vision already coming to fruition. People keep helping me with things: someone lent

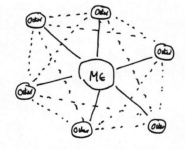

A NETWORK OF
SUPPORTIVE
RELATIONSHIPS

me the Lou Tice tapes, someone else lent me some NLP tapes, another client is teaming up with me to write an article and lead a conference session. Today, in the post, we received a nice letter plus some gifts from Di in Aussieland.

Tuesday 15 March 1994

During a discussion with Barry I realized the importance of operating in line with my values. When I do, I gain in self-respect.

Value through operating in line with your values
The cost of operating in contradiction to my values is an erosion of self-respect and a build-up of stress; each situation becomes volatile, bringing the possibility of unpredictable events (like the angry explosion last year with Edward).

SELF-RESPECT

Thursday 17 March 1994

AMED course entitled 'Challenging Assumptions'. We were asked at the outset to state briefly our 'purpose as a consultant'. I have been working on this question for years, so I was taken aback to be asked to produce an answer in a couple of minutes!

I realized that there are three strong and motivating images/feelings that guide me in my work:

- the image of a pyramid – massive collective human

PROJECT: LIFE CHANGING DEVELOPMENT – R&D	OCT	NOV	DEC	JAN	FEB	MAR	APR	CLIENT: HEALTHCARE COMPANY / ME
1. BRIEFING	▮							
2. ACCELERATED LEARNING COURSE		▮						
3. MARSFIELD CLINICAL COURSE			▮	▮	▮	▮		
4. AMED TRANS. DEVELOPMENT				▮				
5. AMED – CLIENT RELATIONSHIPS					▮			
6. AMED – TRANSITIONS					▮			
7. WRITE & PRESENT REPORT				▦▦▦				
8. PERSONAL DEVELOP METHOD						▮		
9. AMED – CHALLENGING ASSUMPTIONS						▮		

LIFE CHANGING DEVELOPMENT PROJECT

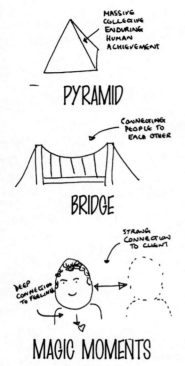

PYRAMID

MASSIVE COLLECTIVE ENDURING HUMAN ACHIEVEMENT

BRIDGE

CONNECTING PEOPLE TO EACH OTHER

MAGIC MOMENTS

STRONG CONNECTION TO CLIENT

DEEP CONNECTION TO FEELING

achievement that stands the test of time
- the image of a bridge — connecting people to each other
- the feeling of magic moments (or bliss) — in which time is elastic, when I am simultaneously connected both inside with my feelings and outside to my client.

These pictures/feelings get me out of a loop of endless wordy intellectualizing and give me a stable direction.

In a later discussion a participant burst into tears. This was bizarre, unbelievable but real. When she recovered, we learned that her behaviour had been spontaneous, but she was upset and I suppose 'blocked' by the group's mode of discussion: it was intellectual without much emotion in it. As I considered what had happened, I connected with a deeply personal issue: I intellectualize, I am guarded with people, I build a protective wall that holds people at a distance, I do not let my emotions show until I really know someone.

After this, my partner in pairwork helped me to recognize when I become animated and seem to be connected with my feelings. I realized there is a moment I sometimes experience in which everything becomes very clear to me. It happens in real time, usually when I am in the company of my client. I feel it is a shared experience, a meeting of minds. In that instant great things seem possible. I have experienced this recently in some client meetings.

I also realized that a 'magic moment' can happen quite quickly with a client, provided the conditions are right. One had just happened to me with someone I had only spoken to for less than an hour! It does not take years of trust-building.

Value through magic moments

The magic moments insights were key to my future thinking about special conversations and Flow Theory. In these moments there is a fuller personal presence in a discussion: it is more than intellectual argument, more than a problem-solving — certainly not a debate or attempt to win a point. It is a total exposure of being, expressing me as I am, feelings and all, which is often accompanied by a new and valuable insight.

Wednesday 23 March 1994

Helen's handbag was stolen. She put it down by the open front door while she nipped back for something. At first we didn't believe it: we hunted around before we accepted it had gone. I took Tom and Georgia to school while Helen sorted things out with the police.

Later on, a client in the healthcare company told me he has never really had a coach or mentor. He seemed to be looking for this but I am falling short: I do not confront him firmly enough, or push him hard enough.

He sees me as highly disciplined and organized. He says he lacks self-organization. But in other ways we are quite similar: both driven by task and at the same time aware of relationships. We both lack personal congruence (what we know versus how we behave) on some level.

He seemed interested in coaching with someone called Garth, but he would not be able to justify funding this from a corporate budget. This made me feel I have been right not to pursue coaching work directly if a company is not willing to pay for it. He encouraged me to work with Garth too.

Value through sharing personal stuff

Our conversation covered a great deal of ground. The client shared a lot of personal matters with me. We discussed our similarities and differences. It seemed that we could both benefit from some personal coaching sessions. I now realize that this was a turning point in our relationship: a transformation was occurring from the task-focused towards learning- and relationship-focused.

Wednesday 6 April 1994

Haworth, Yorkshire. Breakfast followed by a pleasant walk to Oakworth Hall where the kids played in the caves. Journey back on the steam train. Lunch in the Fleece. Drove to Overton for a trip down the mineshaft in a disused colliery. Our guide was a miner called Jeff. He was facing another cut in hours and pay as the museum itself is facing hard times and is threatened by closure. I was really shocked at the appalling conditions in which miners used to work. Conditions like these existed in other mines until this year when most of the British coalmines closed down.

Value through letting go of the old

I was aware of the old giving way to the new. The new is an unknown quantity. The old is familiar, reassuring and seems pleasant even if aspects are dirty, unpleasant or dangerous. It is painful to let go of something certain, however horrible it is, for something uncertain, unknown and, as yet, non-existent.

Saturday 10 April 1994

Rome. Just Helen and me. Sky blue, mild day. Sightseeing. Collosseum. Ruins. Ice creams: zabaglione flavour for me, something equally sweet and luxurious for Helen.

On the way back in the plane Helen and I worked on some goals together. It was fun doing this. It binds us together. Four years ago sitting on a beach in St Malo, we did this: a simple, almost casual expression of intention and checking of agreement. Since then, unconsciously, the intent became real as our lives unfolded.

But we hit the ground with a bump when we returned to Hampton Wick. As we drew up outside our house we noticed that the front door was boarded up. On closer inspection the door was broken, but no one had gained entry. They must have been frightened off.

We became concerned that Tom and Georgia might be afraid and unsettled. I spent the evening nailing planks of wood to the back of the door to hold it together and making adjustments to the lock positions to keep us safe inside.

Value through understanding emotions

Fear, violation, loss: these were some of our emotions. I

realized that these must also be experienced by people involved in corporate change programmes.

Wednesday 20 April 1994

Computer support client. I went into the meeting without a detailed plan deciding to respond to where he – my client – was.

He is digging himself out of the financial hole. He had a record week of billings, and the household accounts were now organized separately from the business. An unpleasant long hours/low margin training job was behind him. He and his wife have given up smoking, using hypnosis. He had wanted more time before this meeting in order to be able to demonstrate some better results. However, when we reviewed things, there was progress and a clear recovery plan.

COACHING PROJECT

Value through change that sticks
Some signs of movement, but I was uncomfortable. Nothing fundamental had changed to prevent the problem recurring. I had no reason to believe the client would not fall back into the hole I had found him in.

Saturday 23 April 1994

On Saturday morning Georgia and I went off on the 285 bus to Burt's the secondhand bicycle specialists in Hampton Hill. I went in to buy a racing bike costing around £100. I left having bought a mountain bike costing £150 and a bike for Georgia!

At the shop Georgia, who is used to riding with stabilizers, tried a secondhand white bike with wide, white

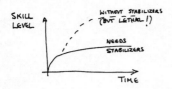

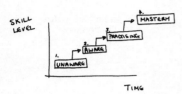

SKILL DEVELOPMENT

tyres. She whizzed up the pavement needing only a little help at first. She had taken an instant step forward up to a new level of skill.

Unfortunately she has not yet learnt to brake and steer so she is lethal. Later she gave us several examples of how she can drive straight into a wall! She is good at pedalling but then she realizes she is going fast, loses her composure, panics, puts her feet down or steers into an obstacle and crashes. If you say 'Mind the wall', she steers straight into it!

Value through high expectations

Before the visit to the bicycle shop I would have said that Georgia cannot ride without stabilizers. I was forced to revise my opinion. From this I learn that development can be faster than we think, that our opinion of others constrains them, that with fast development, comes risk, danger to the person and to others around them. It is exciting, but we need to look after each other.

Wednesday 4 May 1994

While reviewing the end-of-month figures I realized I want to shift my work towards maximum leverage: that is, the most senior level clients, the greatest impact on each client for each consulting day. In consulting-speak this is termed the 'biggest bang for the buck' — a reference to guns rather than sex!

Value through monthly stock-taking

This idea about shifting the work emphasis arose from a number of sources. The end-of-month mini-review of key performance measures helped bring the idea out into a clear expression of intent.

Thursday 5 May 1994

Today I met Garth, a coach recommended to me by a client, in an Italian restaurant in Ealing.

It was not easy to get started. Garth gave me some feedback. I agreed with it. But I was not here today as someone with a particular problem. Garth agreed and the conversation opened right out.

I said that I have difficulty finding people I want to follow: older successful people created how things are today and I want things to be different tomorrow. Our discussion ranged far and wide including the Bible and religion. I had heard that Garth is a Buddhist. He spoke of renunciation, which means 'giving things up'. The other side of this concept is greed which seems endemic today and seems to drive business. Business seems to be today's religion. He sees a disconnect between what organizations say and their true underlying values.

Value through uninhibited discussion
I learnt so much here. I was able to express myself more fully here than almost anywhere else. I did not need to hold anything back. Once something was expressed it seemed to become included in the thought developing between us.

Friday 6 May 1994

The meeting with Garth left me with a good feeling that still remains the following day. The good feeling inside could enable a client to do much more. It builds their confidence, self-esteem and the foundation for top achievement. This good feeling could be what I am seeking to provide in the client relationship, enabling me to manage more relationships and to develop a strategic portfolio of relationships.

Value through being valued
Garth was independent. There was no other agenda. I felt valued, and I felt the power of being valued. I felt the good feeling inside that comes from being valued. I felt that this good feeling could boost my achievement. I sensed this would also be true for other clients.

BEING VALUED

Saturday 7 May 1994

Saturday evening, 6pm. Neighbourhood Watch meeting in Kelly's Dance studio. A challenge for me: I did not want to over- or underprepare. It seemed strange being a self-elected convenor and introducing the meeting. But I was pleased to be able to do this.

20–30 residents came along, also the local PC (nicknamed 'the sheriff') and his sergeant with boxes of pamphlets, stickers and some local crime statistics.

Afterwards Helen said I was a star. I felt a sense of triumph. The scheme was off the ground. The police would be putting up signs. In less than a month from our break-in we had done it.

Value through leading from the front
In this example, as a leader, I was certain of the mutual value of a Neighbourhood Watch scheme, so I proposed and advanced the idea, involving a few others locally. Perhaps that is the difference between leaders and facilitators – certainty, conviction, leading from the front.

Monday 9 May 1994

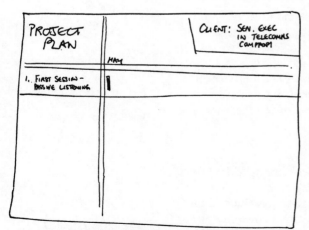

PROJECT PLAN

CLIENT: SEN. EXEC IN TELECOMMS COM PPOPI

MAY

1. FIRST SESSION – PASSIVE LISTENING

EXTERNAL MENTOR PROJECT

Keith was stuck. As a senior management development executive in an international telecommunications company, he had felt compromised by the change programme he had helped his employer to develop. He was now implementing it, but the programme was crumbling around him.

There have been errors. He has been unavailable. He is blaming others. His assistant is unhappy and ready to leave. His projects are mired in politics which he seems unable to resolve.

At our meeting today, he spoke of pain. I detected stress – severe dissonance. He is buried beneath problems and lacking in awareness or sympathy for the pains of the people around him.

He clarified my role as providing external mentor support to him, but warned me there is a sensitivity over the use of consultants and that I must not be too visible.

Value through passive listening

I was one of the few people this client could talk to. I recognized risks in being associated with his failures. But I felt I was being asked to help him. At this time he was just asking me to listen. This seemed too passive, and I started to think about doing something more powerful.

PROGRAMME CRUMBLING

Friday 20 May 1994

A letter arrived from Di who has been working in Macau where she ran the first consulting training for Asian managers in her company. She says it went well, with no cultural disasters despite the varied audience.

She was also pleased that, when masked robbers carrying AK47s robbed the casino below their classroom, they were all sleeping safely in their beds!

Value through training trainers

The value from training I did in 1992 is still spreading and multiplying on the other side of the world!

Monday 30 May 1994

Holiday in Minorca for a week, starting on my 39th birthday.

One day we saw a man jumping from high on the cliffs into the beautiful, clear, blue-green water. Before he jumped the second time we spoke to him. He told us he had dived from just ten feet the previous year into a swimming pool and cut his head open so now he jumps instead of dives.

HOLIDAY

Tom jumped into the pool over 130 times in the space of three days. I played water polo.

Value through stretching the limits
What made him do it? The thrill, I suppose, like bungie jumping – the sense of being free and out of control, the desire to reach beyond the usual limits of your experience.

Tuesday 7 June 1994

A memorable lecture at the Royal Society of Arts by Richard Pascale. He spoke about the proliferation of management fads, about how attempts at transformation fail, about how only approximately five companies worldwide have succeeded, and he lists BA as one. The shift is to 'being' rather than 'doing'. It's about finding something that resonates with all staff: 'the world's favourite airline' is more than an advertising slogan; it carries emotional significance, it resonates with cabin crew and other staff.

He spoke about paradigms as the colour of the light, or 'assumed constants'. Einstein dislodged an assumed constant (time) in favour of another (speed of light). Pascale used powerful imagery: 'trying to drink from a fire hose', 'knowing where you're starting from', 'the karate kid', 'change being both intellectually and emotionally wrenching'.

Value through paradigm shifting
'Paradigms' help to explain 'magic moments'. In the best, most special, generative conversations a person is rearranging their mental furniture, looking at a situation differently, changing the colour of the light. What I have been reaching for is 'what are the conditions that the consultant must create for the client to achieve a paradigm shift that in turn creates enhanced value?'

DRINKING FROM A FIREHOSE

Saturday 11 June 1994

Boat trip down the Thames with my financial adviser, his wife and three daughters, to Kew Bridge and back.

The boat was hard to steer – the response slow. The novice driver (me) tended to overcorrect or make frequent, small, unnecessary movements of the wheel. The boat then zig-zagged down the river. By contrast, the experienced driver fixes their eyes on some stable point on the horizon and moves steadily towards it.

Value through constancy of direction

Steering a boat is a good metaphor for leadership. For several years Page Consulting was zig-zagging. You can also see prime ministers and business leaders doing it.

Sunday 12 June 1994

Last-minute practice for the London to Brighton cycle ride. I cycled into Hampton Court Park, past the 1000-year-old oak tree, past the bustling arrangements for the evening's operatic concert, out on to the River Thames towpath. I monitored speed and distance using the speedo that Helen bought me for my birthday. I did around eight miles (it's 58 miles to Brighton!) and arrived home hot and tired.

Friday 17 June 1994

I am more willing to assert myself than ever before. I am more confident in my work and as a person. I feel on the verge of something – of having total confidence in myself, my values, my personal power and so on. At times I feel a strength, an integrity, a willingness to lead.

I am learning that, when I assert myself, some people will not naturally respond. They may prefer to move away, and that is fine. We are both better off.

LETTING GO

Sunday 19 June 1994

Cycle ride from London to Brighton. I was amongst 25,000 other cyclists, snaking through the traffic-free streets of South London, then country lanes, through villages, past Boy Scouts' barbecues and Women's Institutes' tea stalls. My senses were alive: the sunlight made the colours vibrant. I was alert to sights, sounds and smells. There was an element of danger: a few people fell off and caused accidents. Someone had a heart attack.

For one stretch down a country lane I was behind a girl on a racing bike, who confidently removed her hands from her handlebars. She straightened her back and went on cycling, hands-free, for a while. I cautiously copied.

It was difficult letting go at first, just for a moment, then I grabbed the handlebars again. Each time I tried I was able to travel further. The feeling of straightening my back was wonderful — a relief. The new sense that you develop of how and when to steer through gently leaning the body was a revelation.

Meanwhile — back at the bike ride — I managed to cycle up Ditchling Beacon, the steep hill just before Brighton. It exhausted me, but I felt a great sense of achievement.

Value through letting go

My hands-free cycling taught me about letting go; it was a crucial lesson in facilitation, leadership and personal change. When you let go, you think you will lose control and collapse, but in fact you can achieve a different kind of control — a new relationship with your environment. A stronger, shared control seems to emerge.

Wednesday 29 June 1994

Spent the morning at my office producing a document called 'Designing Education In The Corporate Change Programme'. I was excited about writing down everything I had learned on this topic through hard experience over the last 12 months or so. I was, at the same time, concerned that doing this would make me dispensable.

Value through sharing your knowledge base

At some point, unless the consultant writes down their secrets and gives them to the client they become trapped in a time warp. I could have continued to find instructional design jobs to do, and be well paid for them, but this felt like travelling up a cul de sac. I wanted to rise up to a higher level of consulting. By writing my secrets down I could delegate, hand over and brief others to do instructional design. I became free to meet new opportunities.

SHARING YOUR KNOWLEDGE BASE

Thursday 30 June 1994

Session with Garth. We coached each other. From this I learned to think more about who I help and who I ignore: I tend to think much more about the client personally than the people they affect. This is to do with what Garth calls 'developing compassion'. I also learned to do more confronting, playing devil's advocate and getting people to face contradictions.

Value through co-coaching

Learning took place on two levels here. I learned first from being coached and then from coaching Garth. We gave each other feedback on the experience of being coached.

Saturday 2 July 1994

Discussion with my sister-in-law. She feels our family are too polite, reluctant to hurt one another's feelings and are not communicating well. She suggested a new family motto: 'direct and honest'. I said that politeness is very ingrained, but I will try. I identified something currently that I have been afraid to mention to her: I told her and we dealt with it.

NOTICING AN INGRAINED HABIT

Value through noticing habits and patterns

I began to notice my personal pattern of avoiding conflict. I know the theory of assertion and I have practised the skill of confronting, but I was finding the pattern quite deeply embedded in me, my family and in my upbringing. It was stubborn, resistant to change. I wanted to change it both for professional and personal reasons. Noticing the pattern is the first step to changing it.

Monday 4 July 1994

I have a backlog of past avoidances to put right. All my relationships contain multiple strands of shared history, disagreements, accommodations, unfinished business and, in my case, avoidances and their consequences.

I started writing out some feedback for one client. Then I moved on to Keith. As I did this, I found that I really have been indirect, not honestly owning and feeding back my experience in these relationships. I wanted to do something with this feedback.

In the evening my first chance came when my computer support client faxed me a presentation. After helping him with it, I tested his intentions about my continuing help. He said he wants to get back to our sessions. But I sensed low commitment. I smelled avoidance: he was falling back towards stuckness. I confronted him with my concerns:

- You are using me as your conscience and are not taking responsibility yourself.
- You are becoming immersed in work, leaving nothing else in your life.
- You are at a classic coincidence of pressure points – starting a family and starting a business at the same time.
- This is no good for your wife and, if this continues, she will leave.

This led to a long conversation. He could not see what

he could do. He was not in control of work. There were no decisions, except to survive. There used to be £200 risks and now it was nearer £5000. He recognized his tunnel vision. He had always been like this. It is the way he drives a car; he is not good at moderation. It is difficult being a human being. He wished someone could give him a manual!

We went on until 11.15pm. He summarized my message: he was immersed in work, work had taken over, the costs were going to be very high. I said I had wanted to confront him with this even if it was painful. He said it was not painful, he was already aware of what I was saying. He intended to check with his wife whether he was pursuing a shared plan. I said try using 'What do you want us to achieve together?' instead of 'Here's the plan, do you agree?'.

I felt tired at the end. Helen had gone to bed. My brain was buzzing, and this continued through the night. I was very pleased I had confronted the client; I had been direct with him about what I was experiencing in our relationship.

Value through confronting the client

This was an important confrontation. I was being direct and honest; I was not avoiding. Had I not done this the client would have been entitled to believe that I was supporting him in messing up his life. That would be a dishonest collusion. The quality of the discussion was deep, intense but different from the 'magic moments'. Client and consultant preserved a challenging distance from one another. It was less a process of creation and more one of prodding, testing, blocking escape routes, keeping to the subject.

Tuesday 5 July 1994

When I woke up Helen said 'How is Dr Anthony Clare this morning?'. Had I sorted the client out? I said probably not. I had confronted him with my view but it was probably not sufficient to bring about change. So now I'm thinking about sending personal development tapes and a few other goodies to provide him with a 'manual for life'. I also sent him a fax containing my written feedback.

Later he sent me a fax thanking me for my help with today's presentation. I sent him a 'good luck' fax.

Value through holding the gains

I have since realized that clients slip back. They need help to hold their gains. This comes in the form of questions, checking up, sending prompts and reminders.

By the way, the client's presentation was a competitive tender to an education authority. He won it and, in 1995, they commissioned a £53,000 computer contract from him. Our coaching sessions and our direct work on the presentation played a part in achieving this result.

Wednesday 6 July 1994

I booked up monthly meetings with Keith through to the end of the year. Then I (boldly) sent off the feedback I had written a couple of days ago. It took time to prepare. I felt both pleased and a little scared by the honesty of the result.

I reminded myself that he had asked for feedback. It is balanced. It contains positive points but also plenty of negative ones. It is constructive criticism.

Value through courage

Sending the feedback required courage. It risked destroying a relationship, but it could also move it forward.

Monday 11 July 1994

Monthly coaching meeting with Keith. It had a difficult start. He was on the defensive — asking questions about my role. I sensed a lack of trust. Then we moved into the feedback discussion. He remembered he had asked me for feedback but was taken aback when he received it: he found it cold.

He did not agree with all that I had said. We only had time to look briefly at one item of feedback. At the end of our meeting he was still guarded but agreed to a further meeting to finish what we had started.

PROJECT PLAN — CLIENT: SEN. EXEC IN TELECOMMS COMPANY

	MAY	JUN	JUL	AUG	SEP	OCT	NOV	DEC
1. First Session – Passive Listening								
2. Sent Written Feedback								
3. Session to Discuss Feedback								

EXTERNAL MENTOR PROJECT

Value through face-to-face dealings

In one sense, the delivery of written feedback prior to our meeting was a mistake and set us back. But it did test us. It shook me out of a previous passive listening mode and moved our relationship on.

Wednesday 13 July 1994

Tom's school performance of 'The Emperor and the Nightingale'. He was a peasant in a brown garb made from a pillowcase. He sang peasant songs, played the recorder and sang in a round. At the close the kids filed round the hall carrying their self-made Chinese lanterns, and Mrs Palmer, the new head teacher, made a short speech in which she thanked everyone. I still get shivers down my spine when I hear appreciation. It is so rare. It makes me melt and I see it having the same effect on others.

I've just read sections on feedback in various books. On top of the usual stuff about how to structure the message (e.g. BEST: Behaviour, Effects, Specify alternatives, Talk about outcomes), I reached some conclusions about the meeting process:

- Only one or two critical issues are needed for a one-hour meeting.

- Be brief in the delivery, leaving time for the client to respond.
- Feedback stimulates resistance.
- Gain client reaction before making suggestions.
- Where you sense tension, move towards it, not away from it.
- Contract carefully and check regularly with the client.

I remembered how important it is to leave the client with a good feeling and noticed how easy it would be to leave a sense of confusion or self-hate.

'How are you feeling today?' is an important opening question to check readiness. If the answer is 'pretty lousy' then the feedback session should be postponed. Unfortunately, for some clients, the answer might be 'pretty lousy' every day!

This work made me think about the 'proposition' I can make to clients about the feedback process. It goes something like this:

When I work with you and your people

- you learn from what happens in our relationship
- I give you feedback
- we work through the feedback and both learn from it
- my aim is to help you to fulfil yourself.

The process is challenging, exciting and energizing. As a result

- you enhance your own sense of accomplishment, your personal power and your relationships
- your work improves, you generate greater value for your company.

The value of this method of working can be offered to people throughout your organization.

Value through feedback

A great deal seemed to come clear today. The feedback meeting process and the proposition still seem good to me.

Thursday 14 July 1994

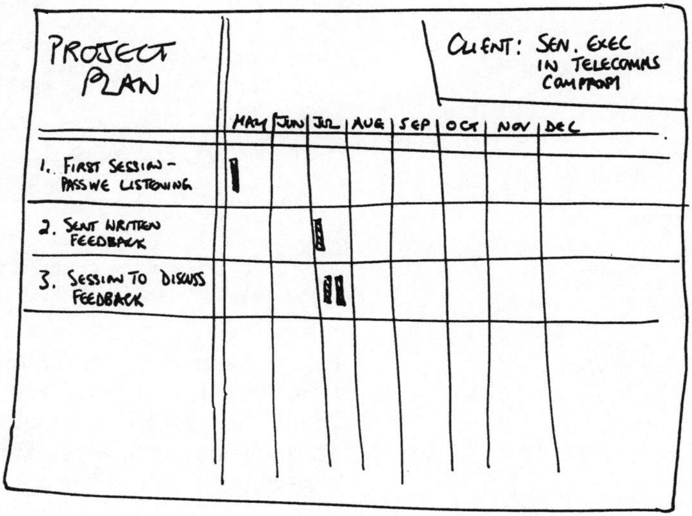
PROJECT PLAN
CLIENT: SEN. EXEC IN TELECOMMS COMPANY
MAY JUN JUL AUG SEP OCT NOV DEC
1. FIRST SESSION – PASSIVE LISTENING
2. SENT WRITTEN FEEDBACK
3. SESSION TO DISCUSS FEEDBACK

EXTERNAL MENTOR PROJECT

In the car, before my meeting with Keith, I took a few moments to 'focus' myself. I wanted to be direct and honest, to hold firmly to my perceptions, and not to avoid or collude.

When we started, Keith asked me why I was doing this. He said no one had previously provided him with feedback in this detail. I said that I was receiving a mixed message: that he is wanting and, at the same time, not wanting feedback. We discussed the kind of feedback he would find most useful.

The meeting exceeded my highest expectations. I was clear about my purpose – honest, direct. I felt able to give my views, comment, highlight contradictions and give direction. Both my relationship with Keith and his own self-awareness seemed to move forward dramatically. At the end of the session he was close to some important decisions.

We did not finish so booked a time next Tuesday to complete. I gained very positive feedback from Keith both during and at the end of the meeting. I became excited about the potential for this feedback process with others as a central tool in managing change.

Value through holding the gains

I read this now and I wonder what went wrong. Much was achieved in this meeting. The confidences expressed

A FEW MOMENTS TO 'FOCUS' MYSELF

by the client were honest; his commitment felt real at the time. But this meeting was not enough to bring about change. Slipping back is a big danger. Holding the gains an enormous challenge. This will become plain as you read on.

Friday 15 July 1994

A phone call last night from computer support client. His tone was up, there was energy in his voice. Good. I also spoke to his wife. The fax had worked dramatically. He is being super-attentive to her. He had had his hair cut: it was shoulder length now it is short. I asked her, should I send another fax to say lay off, cool it? She said no, but she is not sure how long the effect will last.

YES!! I am so pleased to get through.

Today I had an insight. After two successes with client feedback I feel connected and strong. It feels right. I am being nourished by the people I meet and they are being nourished by me. The feedback process is central to my work in managing change. It is all about the individual and their adjustment to their life and their work. It is about individuals discovering their true strength and power. It is about organizations and teams becoming strong, about building world-class organizations, about bringing humanity back in and reintegrating human values into the workplace, replacing exploitative 'Rambo' values with something self-sustaining and nourishing, about making organizations into places where intelligent, sensitive, gifted individuals wish to go on working and spending their lives.

Value through capturing insights

Now I look back on the insight above and I think, yes, that captured something important. It was how I felt at the time and gives me clues about the direction in which I am heading. For me it acts like the stable point on the horizon you need to fix on to steer a boat.

Tuesday 19 July 1994

Keith called me out of a meeting and explained he was running late and unable to attend the feedback meeting we had planned at 5pm. I felt disappointed but I believed Keith was genuinely pressurized and was not avoiding. I believe he wants to complete the feedback process we have started.

Value through not accepting the client's excuses

In fact, this was the first sign of slipping back, but I did not recognize it at the time. I accepted the excuse as genuine. If I had challenged Keith's commitment at this point by perhaps saying: 'On the one hand you are saying this is important and on the other you are cancelling our meeting . . .', then the outcome may have been different. Once I let this excuse pass, it proved very difficult to hold on to the gains with this client.

Thursday 21 July 1994

Joe and I spent a day developing our approach to 'managing change'. We were creating something together. It was exciting. Our style of working was markedly different from last year. Joe had only a rough set of ideas. We took lots of time to share and explore our thinking. Joe refused to rush forward into planning and implementation. First we had to create and believe completely in the concept.

Value through learning and changing
We seemed to be learning from our experience last year and forging a new approach.

Monday 25 July 1994

My expectation was that today's course in Scotland will move me forward another step in my personal development. My fear was that I could get absorbed into a strange and sinister world that distances me from Helen, Tom and Georgia. My hope was that somehow it welds me and my clients into a strong team that has power, integrity and the will to transform an entire organization. Big ambition, huh?

Got up at 5am, taxi at 5.20am, caught the 6.20am train from Euston to Carlisle. Met Joe on the train. We reflected on our work over the last 15 months or so. He asked for some feedback. I gave him some which he said was spot on. We were deep in this conversation. It was easy to forget we were now riding in a taxi up a rocky, muddy path . . . until we were interrupted. We had to keep getting out to open gates. There was more to discuss, but the opportunity passed.

We arrived at a white house surrounded by trees. We met Garth, Leah and Barbara. Then Richard arrived. We walked across the yard behind a barn to a caravan to meet a Buddhist monk in purple robes called Tharchin. He had a smiling face, short, grey crew-cut hair. There was a card on his mirror saying 'I might die today'.

During the day I took sessions on the Alexander Technique: meditation, aromatherapy massage and Buddhist teachings.

I learnt about karmic cycles: you get back in the end what you give out (but not necessarily in this lifetime). If you give out anger and aggression, it takes root in others and comes back to you later.

I MIGHT DIE TODAY

	OCT	NOV	DEC	JAN	FEB	MAR	APR	MAY	JUN	JUL	AUG	SEP	OCT
1. BRIEFING	▌												
2. ACCELERATED LEARNING COARSE		▌											
3. MARESFIELD CURNOW COARSE		▌		▌	▌	▌							
4. AMED TRANS. DEVELOPMENT			▌										
5. AMED – CLIENT RELATIONSHIPS				▌									
6. AMED – TRANSITIONS					▌								
7. WRITE & PRESENT REPORT				▨▨▨▨									
8. PERSONAL DEVELOP METHOD							▌						
9. AMED – CHALLENGING ASSUMPTIONS						▌							
10. THARPALAND COARSE										▌			

PROJECT: LIFE CHANGING DEVELOPMENT – RAD

CLIENT: ~~HEALTHCARE COMPANY~~ ME

LIFE CHANGING DEVELOPMENT

We explored the Buddhist notion of emptiness in which objects have no existence 'of themselves'. Objects are all manifestations of our minds. Through language we gain shared experiences with others. Our relationship to objects is as mother, creator. They come from us; we love and protect them. This attitude is Wisdom. To impute that objects have an existence independent of us is Ignorance, the opposite of Wisdom.

Value through ancient teachings
At the outset this all seemed like nonsense, but it makes more sense as I write about it. Of course I exist as an object in my mind and in other people's minds: this is subjective but real to me and to others. Scientific training has taught us to be objective, to look at reality. From the subjective (Buddhist) viewpoint, you can learn much more about effective and productive relationships, about beliefs, behaviour and about change.

Value through looking after body and mind
The Alexander Technique, aromatherapy and meditation sessions served to raise my awareness of the physical and mental effects of stress. I came to realize the importance of looking after myself.

Tuesday 26 July 1994

Phoned Helen at 7.15am. She seemed happy. Last night's party with the neighbours was fun. The kids played in the garden in their pyjamas until late evening. By contrast, today in Scotland it is raining and windy. The clear view from the front window is obscured by mist and rain.

I am learning a lot. When I listen, I often accept what clients tell me as true, but this is not really the truth: it is a set of 'correct assumptions' or 'givens'. If I don't check, these will descend later into doubts. Meditation is a means of investigation that leads to insight and realization – that is, 'true knowledge'.

Meditation helps you reach the truth by finding 'valid minds' called 'Inferences' and 'Direct Perceivers'. To see something directly is like an 'Aha!', a 'Wow!', a 'Eureka!' or Newton's apple experience.

MEDITATING TO SEE TRUTH

Wednesday 27 July 1994

8.00am meditation, 8.30am a run up the hill with Richard, then a healthy breakfast with food like muesli, yoghurt, sugarless jam, soya milk etc.

After breakfast we had teachings with Tharchin on Attachment, Equanimity and Anger and learned how anger is the most powerful destroyer of achievements in our present and future lives. We meditated on Equanimity in which we put people into three boxes: those we are attached to, those we are neutral towards, those we feel an aversion to. Then we moved people from the attached and aversion box into the neutral.

Thursday 28 July 1994

7.30am. I am losing my sense of what is normal and what is strange. Last night we listened to a tape by an Indian doctor called Chopra, spelling out the limits of the Western medical model and the future possibilities for mind–body medicine. He demonstrated how the body manufactures its own pharmaceuticals. I am still thinking about this.

I am disappointed by the 'one-way' nature of many meditations: like church prayers, I am being fed the lines. Buddhism is not for me. Living daily life in line with non-attachment, loving and compassion is OK and good news because it produces happiness in life. I am told that through 'moral discipline' I can lead a happy life in which I receive a positive feeling from my karmic cycles. If I want to break out of the cyclic existence of birth, marriage, illness and death then I must take the path towards enlightenment but I do not feel inclined to do this!

After lunch, we went to the Gompa (mini-temple) in a converted barn. Participated in an extended meditation on the experience of death: several stages, each of them described in great detail, what is happening to your body, the stench, your consciousness, the lights. This drew on the real death experiences of Buddhists over hundreds of years.

MEDITATION ON DEATH

Afterwards we were asked to reflect on 'What will I regret if I died today?'. Garth said that whenever I talk about home, it is all warm and 'squidgy' stuff but when I speak about work it is cold, arid, structured and formal. He said I am like a knight on a white horse, all ready but without a cause, without a battle to fight. This contradiction signals something still incomplete in my life.

Friday 29 July 1994

Reflexology: my feet were massaged and manipulated to gauge my overall health and well-being. Final session with Tharchin in which he referred to the subtle body, chakras, tantra and other tantalizing mysteries that we had not had time to look at.

Before lunch Garth ran a session in which we discussed the issues surrounding individuals, the company and the planet. We concluded that:

- the company can be viewed as an entity, creating its own karmic cycles
- a company is really just a collection of people; all of these people changing can bring about change in the company
- a corporate change programme must be non-religious enabling all compassionate people to enlist — Christians, Muslims, Buddhists and atheists
- we should develop people to bring out their compassion, to transform the company to bring about positive action in the world.

After lunch a group photograph and a one and a half hour drive to Glasgow, then the BA shuttle to London. Picked up the kids at 6pm.

In the evening I talked with Helen about the course. She felt conned. She felt I had been conned. She asked how much the course cost. I had gone away on a jolly, while she was left with the kids. It was as if Helen felt a little threatened by it. Had I actually taken a big risk?

Could my mind have been overtaken by aliens? I remembered my earlier resolve to discuss this course with Helen and only to go with her consent. I did not do this. The discussion would have raised unanswerable questions about the course, the value of it and so on. I had trusted my colleagues not to take me into dangerous territory.

Value through holding fire

Once Helen had expressed her concerns about Tharpa they seemed to evaporate. I chose not to labour the subject after this. I hoped that events in the coming months might demonstrate to Helen benefits in me and in our relationship. I did not need to be right about this. I chose to wait and see.

Value through trusting

The trust did pay off. Tharpa was a powerful but totally benign influence. I discovered more about myself. I strengthened relationships with my colleagues. I gave feedback to Joe and to Richard. I moved my relationship forward with both of them from 'doer' to something like a 'trusted and equal partner'.

Monday 1 August 1994

Haworth, Yorkshire. The kids pressed me to take them up on the hills before breakfast to do some more drawing. The weather was good for Pennine country. We looked at mists hanging over hills. We saw the profile of the hills emerging as the sun evaporated the mist. We played in the heather. We followed footprints. We found berries. Georgia and I sat on one side of a disused rock quarry crater while Tom ran round to the other and back through the middle. Fun together, exercise, fresh air, stimulation, learning about plants, hills, quarries, windmills, winds etc. Bliss!

PLANNERS' REMORSE

Tuesday 9 August 1994

Meeting at the Strategic Planning Society in Portland Place. There were 15-minute presentations on corporate change and re-engineering. I noticed a surprising remorse amongst some older planners present for their part in downsizing companies over the last decade or so. They were raising such questions as 'Where will the jobs for our children come from?'.

When I got back I mentioned this to my nephew who is studying engineering at Hull. He told me he had just spent eight weeks doing lectures on 'how to design products to minimize human input and error'. On the ninth week the lecturer asked them, 'What do we do about all the people thrown out of work?'. He did not present any answers, and his class felt that the last eight weeks had been rather wasted. This dilemma is still unresolved.

Value through trusting relationships
I reflected on this afterwards. People have been thrown out of jobs because, relative to machines, they can be costly and unreliable. The mutual trust that perhaps once existed between employer and employee has broken down. This is a breakdown in the value equation. Underlying the job creation question are two further questions: 'How do we re-build the trust?' and 'How can employees create the highest added value in a slimmed-down, efficient business?'

Thursday 18 August 1994

I met Brian, a healthcare client, to look at 'education' in the company, ten years hence. It turned out to be a remarkable meeting.

I took the role of questioning him, capturing what he said using mind maps on the flipchart. It was slow, boring and predictable at first. I asked about vision. We spoke of continuous learning and plans for a company university. I asked what would make the company better than its competitors. The list was predictable at first: leadership, managing change, learning, etc. – old hackneyed stuff. Then some distinctive items began to appear: working as one, thinking as one, continually learning and adapting like the HIV virus.

We asked what it would feel like working for the company in ten years' time. The answers: when you enter the workplace you would sense that it is different; there would be an intense feeling of engagement at work – it is you and you are it. All of your senses would be engaged.

We envisaged self-directed teams enabling personal awareness, enabling freedom to exercise choice, enabling people to align themselves to their preferred role. There would be direct employee awareness of the bottom line, a sense of my time, my money, my success, losing the barriers, a personal stake in business success. Education would help to connect people in the business. Education would be 'the great aligner'.

A GENERATIVE CONVERSATION

It seemed unstoppable. We moved into bigger questions such as bringing the learning organization to life, the quality of relationship between company and individual, the benefits of small teams. We found that company success hinges on its understanding of human nature. Brian asked provocatively, 'Would you open dog kennels without understanding the basic needs of dogs for space, food, light etc?' Human nature is largely ignored by companies. Companies must respect people's inner space in return for getting performance and commitment.

At around this point we stopped. The intense adrenaline rush, the racing stream of thoughts began to settle. I felt tiredness spreading through my brain. We had been in discussion for over two hours without a break. Brian and I were both rather dazed – amazed at what we had come out with and a little confused about what to do with it. I agreed to take the flipcharts and get them typed up to review later. Afterwards I realized that neither of us could have produced this material alone. There was a unique value generated here from client and consultant, working together in a special way.

Value through a generative conversation

This meeting illustrates a 'generative' conversation in which client and consultant build on one another's ideas to produce something entirely new. What they produce together has a potent effect, bringing about a change of viewpoint in both the client and the consultant.

Wednesday 24 August 1994

EXPERT CONSULTATION

I took Tom to hospital for a consultant's appointment to check out the lump on his neck. We cycled there and arrived dead on time at 11.30am. Waiting was a bit irritating, and the receptionist did not treat seriously my need to know when we would actually get in to see the consultant. She wasn't obstructive but just unaware of my time pressures. I felt I was being pushy but when she offered the opportunity to queue-jump I declined. It did not seem fair.

When we got in to see the consultant he was quite relaxed. He kept me informed while he put Tom at his ease. I was asked questions about Tom's health from birth onwards and then we discussed the lumps in Tom's neck, when they appeared etc. He spent a long time feeling the lumps and later examining Tom's chest, underarms and groin for signs of other swollen glands.

When the questions and examination were complete he clearly explained his diagnosis: three lumps not just one, an after-effect of some viral infection, not anything malignant to worry about. He needed to make a routine check on Tom's blood count and will leave a message to confirm all is OK on the answerphone.

I was pleased, my load felt lighter, we cycled back through Kingston and bought a Burger King lunch for Tom and a Burger King toy for Georgia.

Value through expert consultation

This was an exemplary expert consultation: the consultant put us at ease, drew from both of us contextual and specific information, completed a physical examination of the whole body system, arrived at a diagnosis, communicated it to the patient, described/ advised the next steps.

The patient (client) is engaged at a minimal level only, made to feel relaxed and willing to undergo examination, allowed to ask questions at the end, expected to accept both diagnosis and recommended next steps. The expert's body of knowledge is kept secret from the client.

There is a higher form of collaboration possible between client and consultant. Neither has the answer (because we live in a world of enormous complexity), the client has some data, the consultant brings methods, impartiality and perspective. Client and consultant engage as equals, together sharing existing information to generate new and original solutions.

Thursday 25 August 1994

Helen returned from a two-day trip to Holland around 6pm and helped to thaw the ice that had built up between me, the kids and their teenage cousins who were acting as childminders. She went to us each in turn (kids, childminders and me) and gently but persistently enquired about how we have all got on while she had been away. There was sympathy for each of us when she found out how fraught it had all become.

Value through a gentle touch
Helen's light touch was most effective. It seemed magically to transform how we all felt. Within a few minutes the others were helping me to wash the car!

Sunday 28 August 1994

The 'repas annual and petanque championship' took place on the bank of the River Garonne in South West France. A blue and white canopy was pitched just on the edge of the river with long laid tables and benches. People were milling around drinking aperitifs. Our kids were timid, put off by all the French speaking and the strange setting (we had only arrived from England the previous day).

The meal lasted around three hours: melon, roast lamb from the barbecue, apples, nectarines, cheese and coffee, lots of local wine and fresh bread. We were made to feel very welcome. People had time for us despite our inability to speak their language properly. Monsieur Breil persuaded me to enter the petanque competition.

I surprised myself and Helen by chatting to a chap called Paul sitting alone on the next table whom I knew to be English. This kind of extrovert advance is most uncharacteristic of me, but it felt quite easy and natural on this occasion. Paul had just gained a petanque licence and helped me with the formalities of enrolling in the competition.

The surfaces were uneven – rough gravel and broken asphalt. The irregularity helps to handicap the better players, making the result less predictable. Neither of my partners was an expert. One was the mayor of the village. Both were generous with their advice but less than expert at playing. They were tolerant but a little tested by an Englishman who hardly spoke their language. We used sign language most of the time.

My team lost. There were 16 cups waiting to be awarded but after two hours or so of play and being knocked out we left to return to the cottage.

Wonderful day, testing our French, acclimatizing us and the kids. By the time we left Georgia had settled in with some French kids playing happily with old bottle tops.

Value through finding a clear intention

Recently in social situations I had been in a repeating pattern of mixed-up emotions, a confusion of approach and avoidance. But, through reflection, I had discovered my intention to be relaxed socially which seemed to have resulted in exactly that behaviour. When the behaviour came it was natural, comfortable and appropriate. I felt good. It was like getting a result, almost without trying. No hard work was involved. This was intention translating easily and unconsciously into behaviour change.

Tuesday 6 September 1994

Back to work. A start-up meeting with Richard and Peter. We discussed the re-engineering project which Richard is leading. They have realized that the greatest single risk to total success is 'change management'. Everyone involved with and affected by the project needs to be able to manage change.

We discussed how 'change management' is all about people and how they feel during a programme of change. At the end, I felt sure they both understood the importance of addressing the human dynamic, including issues such as honesty, threat, insecurity and well-being.

The new CEO in a client company is buying and selling companies. So far he has acquired a healthcare group and a pharmaceutical company. Recently he sold an existing business unit. I sensed in the people there a positive excitement about restructuring but also concerns.

How would it affect jobs? The spread of plants throughout the world reflected history rather than manufacturing logic, so would factories close? With the acquisition came talented people but would they all be needed? In places there were two people for every job. Who would go?

Selling the business unit displayed a certain attitude to the people working within it. It was the severance of an established relationship — cutting off a member of the family. It is head put before the heart: perhaps rational and necessary but still unpleasant. What feelings do the people remaining have? A greater sense of security because someone is building the business strongly, but perhaps diminished self-worth because, like commodities, they are vulnerable to the tides of corporate logic, fashion, expediency and necessity.

PROJECT PLAN — SEPT — CLIENT: HEALTHCARE COMPANY — 1. START-UP MEETING

CHANGE MANAGEMENT PRODUCT DEVELOPMENT PROJECT

WE'VE SOLD B DIVISION FOR $1bn!

CEO

HE'D SELL HIS GRANDMOTHER FOR 50p

READJUSTING EXPECTATIONS

Value through addressing the human dimension in change

I had recently realized that 'change management' is much less about project management and much more about people and their willingness to participate.

Value through realigning employee expectations

'Survivor syndrome' is the term which describes how the people left working after downsizing are affected. Their relationship to the employer has changed invisibly. They readjust their expectations, commitment and loyalty in the light of their employer's actions.

Wednesday 7 September 1994

Dashed to Hampstead for my meeting with Barry. He asked me a couple of useful questions:

Q: 'What enduring client question do you expect Page Consulting to be answering in the year 2000?'
A: 'Helping organizations facing change to achieve real engagement from their people.'

Q: 'What do you want to achieve by Christmas?'
A: 'Real progress with the Managing Change product and clear plans for it, extension to client base beyond the healthcare company'.

Value through questions of clarification

Answering these questions helped to bring my work into a clearer focus from the swirling mists of possibilities.

Wednesday 14 September 1994

In the evening I set aside 30 minutes and meditated. I noticed two current concerns:

- Real progress in growth and development comes from working on my own assumptions and beliefs.

- Diary or meditation? Both can help me to identify and refute old assumptions and wrong beliefs, but what is the role of each?

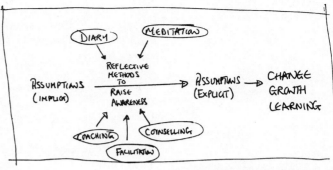

REFLECTIVE METHODS

Afterwards I noted some assumptions and questions I would like to work on:

- Does the end justify the means?
- Does the cause of happiness and suffering lie inside or outside of us?
- Is it better to be self-sufficient than to depend on help from others?

Value through working on assumptions

I now know that my interest in working on underlying assumptions is supported by the views of others, such as Chris Argyris (type 2 learning is about finding the underlying rules that guide our behaviour).

Chaos/complexity theory is also compatible with this. A complex adaptive system (like the Stock Exchange or the drivers on the M25) displays an infinite range and diversity of behaviour that has all been generated by a few simple rules.

Saturday 17 September 1994

For Helen's 40th birthday we wanted a big event. The theme was the Roaring Forties. We had a vision of people milling round on the lawn chatting on a warm summer evening, but the weather has just turned cold.

Everyone had a job to do. I helped collect and put up the marquee. Helen's family arrived early and prepared the food. A nephew acted as wine waiter.

There were 50 or so guests, a mix of friends and family. It turned out well. The atmosphere was buzzing. A string quartet provided Mozart and Vivaldi then we

MARKING AN OCCASION

played CDs of Glenn Miller and 'Larry Adler playing Gerschwin'. Helen's dad was dancing with her mum and each of his daughters in turn. It was the first time for years that my mum, dad and brothers had been together in the same room, and it felt good.

We had unlimited sparkling wine, expensive cheeses, fireworks. It felt like a happy wedding. I noticed others enjoying themselves and I did too.

Value through marking an occasion

All turning up and celebrating Helen's 40th marked it as a positive occasion enjoyed in a multitude of ways by a multitude of people. It was a happy event that we look back to.

Monday 19 September 1994

Monthly meeting with Keith. Unpromising start: he was unsure if we were meeting or not. Apologies — only an hour available instead of two.

Here we were in the middle of September. Our final feedback meeting in July had been cancelled. He exuded stress. He frequently seemed negative and powerless. He had some good ideas, but he could not start anything new without running up against his trainer colleagues in the company. In this sense he was a prisoner, but he was also one of the trainer group playing a jailer — stopping others from stepping out of line, willing to mutter, criticize and moan.

PROJECT PLAN

CLIENT: SEN. EXEC IN TELECOMMS COMPANY

	MAY	JUN	JUL	AUG	SEP	OCT	NOV	DEC
1. FIRST SESSION – PASSIVE LISTENING	I							
2. SENT WRITTEN FEEDBACK			I					
3. SESSION TO DISCUSS FEEDBACK			II					
4. CLIENT POSTPONES MEETING				I				
5. COMMITMENT TESTING MEETING					I			

EXTERNAL MENTOR PROJECT

The meeting seemed to be going round in circles. I offered a choice about whether or not to continue with our sessions. If we do, I said I wanted to be sure we could create some real value.

He said he wanted to continue the monthly meetings, firstly to discuss a specific project and then a second meeting for his personal development afterwards. He said that he did not have anyone else he could talk to in this way.

He went on to explore the difficulties he was having over the reporting relationships. This led him towards his sense of vulnerability: is there a role for him or not? If not would there be a role for him anywhere inside or outside the company?

Value through lowering expectations

My earlier optimism about this client's progress had turned to pessimism during the summer. I was prepared to walk away but persuaded to continue. My expectations from this point onwards were low.

Value through testing commitment

This client's commitment was highly variable and his behaviour unpredictable. The session had become a kind of comfortable haven away from the hostile workplace. If the client is not committed to pursuing value, then sessions like this are a waste of time.

Tuesday 20 September 1994

I was in another meeting when Keith popped his head round the door. He was smiling and his eyes were sparkling. I have never seen him like this. It felt like he was saying 'thank you' for something – perhaps it related back to yesterday's meeting. (Or perhaps he had won the football pools?!).

I was affected by this. Keith usually hides in meetings or at his desk. He does not pop his head round doors. He seemed secure, happy, positive, extrovert. I hardly recognized him. His face was totally different.

OBSERVING THE CLIENT'S ENERGY

Value through observing the client's energy

I felt this change in Keith's demeanour might be a by-product of our coaching sessions: he was extending himself outwards into the world again. It could equally have been that he was having a good day, had received some good news or a burden had lifted or been removed. But the important thing was that his personal energy was different, opening up a new range of possibilities to him.

Wednesday 21 September 1994

I awoke feeling rushed, tired, happy but behind with my work.

The working day started with an 8.20am Vision Workshop with the re-engineering team. Richard introduced it, showed a Joel Barker video, talked about Lou Tice and Accelerated Learning, then pitched me in to lead a short meditation – relaxation with eyes closed and baroque music, then visioning the team's future state.

This was quite a daring and risky workshop design, although not a bad team to try it out on. I felt exposed because I had not previously led a meditation process. I did not know how long to allow for each part or how much to talk. Richard told me afterwards I was speaking too much. Someone else said she liked my voice and that she enjoyed it, but she was amazed we were able to do anything of this kind within a corporate environment.

We went on to capture and develop a great many thoughts on vision. At the end of this the team members were rather confused, but I was finding a clear set of ideas crystallizing in my mind. I started to share these with the team.

PROJECT PLAN	SEPT	CLIENT : HEALTHCARE COMPANY
1. START-UP MEETING	8	
2. VISION VALUES WORKSHOP	1	

CHANGE MANAGEMENT PRODUCT DEVELOPMENT PROJECT

We did some work on values before lunch. I asked various questions, people wrote down their values and then each person was given a couple of minutes to describe their values to the group. We did not debate these because values represent deeply-held beliefs that are not amenable to change. The purpose was simply for everyone to know what other people's values were. I made notes on the electronic whiteboard and gave everyone a copy.

Value through stretching into new areas

This session was a big risk for me, since it stretched me beyond what I was normally happy to do. It will take time before we really know the effects of doing this session, but I have a feeling that personal development, meditation and advanced learning techniques are being seen as less 'way-out' and more acceptable.

My view? These methods are being embraced in the sporting world where the link between personal preparation, team alignment and results is clearly demonstrable. If they create value then you better start using them or you'll be left behind!

Monday 26 September 1994

Running a course for management consultancy firm at Latimer House. My bedroom is central and set high in the house, overlooking field, lakes and forest.

At the start of the day I reminded myself to put the 'means before the ends'. This simple principle causes me to attend to the needs of the participants in the course rather than just rushing to achieve each of the deadlines in

CONSULTANT DEVELOPMENT PROJECT

the programme. Today this certainly seemed to have paid off. You can tell learning is taking place.

Dinner finished around 10.30pm and, at this moment, I am lying in my bed in the beautiful bedroom with my Powerbook on my lap keying in this diary.

Value through putting means before ends
On a course, the 'ends' are 'stated learning objectives achieved within the limits of the timetable'. The 'means' are 'participants actively engaging in learning exercises within a well structured programme'. By being 'means-focused', finding out participants' questions and helping them gain answers during the course, the 'ends' are achieved. If you are 'ends-focused' participants resist, and everyone fails.

Tuesday 27 September 1994

Course day two. According to this morning's national newspapers my client for this course has announced a merger with Arthur Andersen. It seems a strange choice. The larger firm is known for its global reach, its systems, the uniformity of its approach and its people. They have been cruelly nicknamed 'the androids' and have tried to shed their 'clone' image in the consulting industry. By contrast I thought of my client as a smallish UK management consulting firm comprising individuals who would not fit easily into a corporate mould.

Value through keeping doubts to yourself
Now was not the time for me to raise any doubts. The staff needed to go to a briefing session first before making up their own minds.

Wednesday 28 September 1994

Last day of course. Woke up and looked out of the window to see a stunning view of mist hanging over the water in the valley and gradually lifting to reveal a view of boats on water. Good results from course. Pleased to be home, but with familiar sensation of dislocation and strangeness.

Monday 3 October 1994

Facilitator Development course in Scotland. After breakfast, a short walk in Drymen village to get oriented. Breath-taking views of hills around. Mild day with distant sun and a light wind.

We wrote lists in our notebooks: negative thoughts, positive self-images, cravings etc., defining the frame through which we see our world. After lunch we each made presentations on 'who we really are'. I spoke about my sister's death and my parents' divorce. Difficult to talk about in front of ten relative strangers but important. I felt quite emotional.

PROJECT: LIFE CHANGING DEVELOPMENT - R&D
CLIENT: HEALTHCARE COMPANY (ME)

	OCT	NOV	DEC	JAN	FEB	MAR	APR	MAY	JUN	JUL	AUG	SEP	OCT
1. BRIEFING	▮												
2. ACCELERATED LEARNING COURSE		▮											
3. MARESFIELD CURNOW COURSE			▮	▮	▮	▮							
4. AMED TRANS. DEVELOPMENT			▮										
5. AMED – CLIENT RELATIONSHIPS					▮								
6. AMED – TRANSITIONS						▮							
7. WRITE & PRESENT REPORT						▨▨							
8. PERSONAL DEVELOP METHOD								▮					
9. AMED – CHALLENGING ASSUMPTIONS								▮					
10. THARPALAND COURSE										▮			
11. FACILITATOR DEVELOPMENT COURSE													▮

LIFE CHANGING DEVELOPMENT PROJECT

Tuesday 4 October 1994

Today Richard seemed pensive. The course was hitting home. He saw all facilitation as manipulation and recognized how he justifies his manipulation.

After dinner we had a session entitled 'What is

facilitation?". François, one of the tutors, facilitated. We learned that, unless a discussion or meeting is addressing a burning question that really matters to the people present, it is a waste of time. We tried to find ourselves a burning question. We spent one hour proposing questions but there was no consensus. So there was no discussion to be facilitated, and we disbanded for the night.

Wednesday 5 October 1994

Final day of the facilitation course. We spent some time practising and developing our coaching skills.

I volunteered to be coached in a simple task — throwing tennis balls into a bin. I kept missing. I was asked to say where the ball actually fell, how far from the bin and in which direction. My thrill was to come from accurate reporting rather than hitting the bin. The coach was not to praise a good result or comment on a poor one, but simply to ask about the accuracy of my reporting. Gradually and naturally through unconscious body intelligence I started hitting the bin. Pretty soon I got the ball in. The essence of coaching I learned from the task was as follows:

- Discover the client's inner experience of doing the task.
- Find a way to put the client in touch with the reality of what is happening.
- Move the goal from 'winning' to 'staying in touch with reality'.
- Do not try too hard.

When I arrived home Helen told me of momentous decisions she has been taking. She had a 'straw breaking the camel's back' incident at work last week. In the last few days at work she had taken on a decisive 'sod it, just do it' attitude and has been pleased to find the path clearing in front of her. She has also decided to leave Shell.

Value through living in the moment

The course was all about living in the present, being naked emotionally and intellectually, applying no effort, keeping your web of thought 'loose', dancing like a naked baby in wonder and appreciation. It involved not being distracted by memories or by planning or fantasies, nor ever to be doing anything you don't want to; either decide to stop or decide to continue and enjoy it. Be there in the moment.

So why am I still keeping this diary? It's just dead knowledge. It's just memories. No. It frees me. It rids me of guilt. It loosens my web and allows me to regain balance.

Value through making a decision

Once Helen finally made the decision to leave Shell, she was able to make new plans. Her energy was freed from the frustrations of daily working life and could be targeted towards more productive new areas. She gained a new attitude of healthy detachment when at work.

Tuesday 11 October 1994

Meeting with Joe at my office. He has just started in his new role – a big opportunity for him. He has five key focus areas defined with his boss. One is to develop a 'top team process', and he wants help.

We did some good coaching. We discussed how coaching works (using the 'tennis ball in bin' example from last week). We went straight to his burning question, 'Have I taken on too much?'.

The answer we reached was: you are confusing technical and human components of your task. You cannot 'promise' to your boss how people will respond at a forthcoming meeting. That depends on them. You can make sure they own the meeting and that you do not, in subtle unintentional ways, undercut your own success. You can make sure you continue to use honest facilitation rather than manipulation or 'facipulation' and build honest, effective working relationships with them.

I found myself very relaxed and effortlessly adding value. What we were achieving felt strong, certain, good.

Value through getting to the burning question

Getting to the burning question is a way of working at the highest possible value, wasting no time, dealing with the real issues. This was a good start, bringing high motivation to the discussion. We were soon immersed together in the question, and I could sense we were making progress. I felt strong, natural. I did not have to deliberately think or analyse: the right questions came spontaneously to me. There was no anxiety. It was like riding a bike, without your hands on the handlebars, still being able to steer but less directly. My energy and the client's energy were proof it was going well.

Thursday 13 October 1994

Meeting started late. Keith seemed happier, lighter. His boss had announced a postponement of several projects Keith was involved in. He did not feel threatened by this. It freed him to get on with work he felt to be more interesting or important.

Quite spontaneously and easily he seemed to become active, creative. His pen was sketching an idea on the paper in front of him — an enactment of his vision to lead and nurture his people in the business. I could hardly believe the change in him.

I drew the meeting to a close around 5.30pm. I had a very positive feeling. It felt like a turning point. I wondered, though, about the strong negative energy and insecurity still surrounding the other members of his team.

PROJECT PLAN		CLIENT: SEN. EXEC IN TELECOMMS COM PPOPI						
	MAY	JUN	JUL	AUG	SEP	OCT	NOV	DEC
1. FIRST SESSION – PASSIVE LISTENING	I							
2. SENT WRITTEN FEEDBACK			I					
3. SESSION TO DISCUSS FEEDBACK				II				
4. CLIENT POSTPONES MEETING				I				
5. COMMITMENT TESTING MEETING					I			
6. SPONTANEOUS CREATIVE MEETING						I		

EXTERNAL MENTOR PROJECT

Value through removing burdens
This was an astonishing change of mood. A simple piece of news from the boss had caused a huge transformation in Keith.

Friday 14 October 1994

I bumped into Sarah. She has spoken to people from the recent facilitator development course. One tried to explain the course to others but has given up. It is more than he can encompass in words. Sarah herself was depressed afterwards, facing up to a number of things in her life that have not been right over the last year. Len, who was angry, is angry no longer. Instead he is relaxed, unbelievably happy.

I found the course valuable. I feel free of my past, free to live in the present, to give and gain the most from life. I have insights around facilitation which move my own practice forward. I do feel happier, easier, more confident. I am losing my need to hide myself. I am finding what is honest and finding it is more easy to express.

Value through personal development
The discussion with Sarah shows the variety of results that personal development can achieve. We all gained different results. What we each got was a function of what we needed at the time to move us on. The corporation gets many things from it, but you could summarize it as 'people with greater interpersonal awareness and more positive energy'.

Wednesday 19 October 1994

I blew up just when we were all leaving the house at 8am. Tom and Georgia had both been ready in their coats. Georgia pushed Tom against the wall and his rucksack caused him to bounce back into an upright position. So Tom did the same to Georgia. OK so far. But then they repeated it two or three times, gradually putting more

ERUPTION

and more force into the pushing until Georgia bashed her head on the wall and was in tears.

I erupted! A loud shouting, angry voice came out of me, telling Tom off. This amazed and frightened me. It made Tom cry and defend himself saying why should he care about his 'rotten little sister' anyway. The last time I felt such uncontrollable rage was when Edward and I had our one and only argument in January 1993.

Helen was surprised too and afterwards seemed to be dealing with me a little guardedly. She said it was good for Tom, that he is too egocentric. I was worried that I had frightened him.

Later I felt annoyed when a client phoned up to postpone tomorrow's meeting. I did not own up to this. I said I understood his position, which I do. Later a call from Joe on the answerphone also suggested we postpone a meeting.

My work diary is not booked up. This month the billing is poor. Everyone seems guarded and insecure. Jobs are being redefined. Costs are under pressure. Consultants seem a luxury.

Reflections on the explore phase

REFLECTIONS

What was really going on?

I was maintaining a high level of income while developing myself. I delivered some important pieces of education product. I was commissioned by a client to discover and report on 'what's out there' in terms of 'life-changing' personal development.

Initially, I felt my job was simply to understand and report on 'life-changing development' to my client. This gave me a slight distance, but gradually I started to participate more fully in courses and, as a result, I became clearer about what is really important to me. In other words, the courses nourished a personal development process of my own.

By the end I felt my eyes had been opened; a rebalancing had taken place in my life, and I was ready to redefine my approach to work.

What is my theory about why?

What happened in this phase was linked to my continuing search for value and my previous intention to 'be authentic'. My movement towards authenticity had been interrupted by the need to 'fight back' in the previous phase.

This exploratory phase provided an opportunity to question and challenge some deeper assumptions that produced the anxious and inauthentic consultancy behaviour that I wanted to shed.

At first I approached personal development with the focus and drive of a highly task-driven achiever, taking copious notes and working hard to extract meaning from them. This started me actively participating and reflecting.

The learning process was not like a change demanded or imposed on me by any course. It is better described as reminding me what I really want – including what I had wanted all along – raising my awareness about contradictions in my life and work, then helping to remove the contradictions. It took on a momentum of its own.

My eyes were opening to dimensions of life beyond plain project work. I became more aware of my family, my physical health and my personal beliefs. A rebalancing was occurring, which impacted on my work. My work became more like coaching with the client and less 'taking away a job and doing it for the client'. I started to participate more with the client in defining the brief rather than accepting a *fait accompli*. I started to challenge the brief, to delegate work that I was no longer interested in doing. I was willing to walk away rather than do pointless work. I was beginning to work more in line with my personal values.

The after-effects of various development activities were cumulative and were gradually working through into visible life changes. I was becoming less task-driven. I was emerging from a black cloud of isolated serfdom, confusion and guilt into a positive, proactive, confident awareness of interdependency with others. I was coming alive to the underlying human dynamics in work.

In summary, at the end of this phase the transformation is still incomplete: I have explored beyond my previous narrow task-driven focus into the world of relationships and interpersonal dynamics. I still need to discover a balance between task and relationship.

EXERCISE: LOCATING DISSONANCE

Most of us live with some background feelings of discomfort, dissonance and stress. Usually we blot these out, denying they exist, blaming/projecting them on to others and hoping they will pass quickly. This exercise is designed to look for dissonance. Why? Because dissonance is the fuel for transformational learning.

1 **Choose any two 'worlds' from the following list:**

   - business
   - career
   - home life
   - social life
   - local community life
   - personal health and fitness
   - finances
   - self-image.

2 **For each of the two 'worlds' chosen, ask yourself: 'What really matters to me about it?' Write down two or three items on each list.**

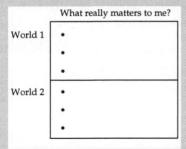

	What really matters to me?
World 1	•
	•
	•
World 2	•
	•
	•

EXERCISE

---

3 Now for each of the two 'worlds' chosen, take a critical look and ask yourself 'What is currently missing?'. Write down two or three items on each list.

	What really matters to me?	What is currently missing?
World 1	• • •	• • •
World 2	• • •	• • •

4 Now look at your answers for any themes, connections, interrelationships and conflicts. Note them here.

5 Repeat the Locating Feelings exercise provided earlier (see p. 24).

Phase 4 Reframe

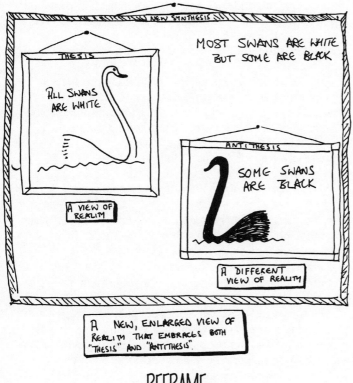

MOST SWANS ARE WHITE
BUT SOME ARE BLACK

THESIS

ALL SWANS
ARE WHITE

A VIEW OF
REALITY

ANTITHESIS

SOME SWANS
ARE BLACK

A DIFFERENT
VIEW OF REALITY

NEW SYNTHESIS

A NEW, ENLARGED VIEW OF
REALITY THAT EMBRACES BOTH
"THESIS" AND "ANTITHESIS".

REFRAME

In the fourth phase of this five-phase journey a whole series of 'new,' but in a sense 'blindingly obvious', insights and realizations came tumbling forth.

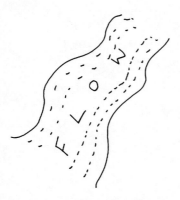

THE HUMAN DIMENSION IN CHANGE

Thursday 20 October 1994

A decisive meeting with Joe. We had started earlier to develop a change management product. We recognized that users would have entry-level questions (wants) but that the product must meet underlying needs. We had prepared lists of users' probable wants and underlying needs to bring to the meeting.

In the meeting we had a series of humbling realizations. First we found that, instead of revealing the user's motivation, the underlying needs list merely revealed our own. Next, we do not have enough experience ourselves to encompass the whole of change management. Any product must grow – evolve from our experience as it accumulates.

And yet another realization: we cannot produce a 'product' in the form of a manual, a CD-ROM or a 'how to' book. We are midwives, not inventing something but bringing life, access, legitimacy and prominence to something that already exists that people are already living. A (blank?) diary is more appropriate.

What could be unique in our work is the full recognition of the human dimension in change which is like water – a flow. You cannot block it, you can channel it, pump it but you must go with it, to go against it is futile. The next humbling realization was the amount of futile manipulation we have been involved in to date as consultants and facilitators. It will be difficult to live without manipulation.

We recognized that our work together is most challenging and exciting when it is offering us personal growth. The best place to start in developing a product would be with our own burning questions, then to document how they evolve.

There has been much excitement generated around complexity theory which seems to be a bunch of scientists in different fields coming to similar conclusions. Why don't we create a label 'Flow Theory' and see what reaction that stimulates? I agreed to start documenting my thoughts and reference sources on Flow

Theory. Meanwhile Joe would start talking into a tape recorder as his form of diary-keeping.

Value through humility

From our willingness to give up on a previous idea, admitting we got it wrong, we created something real, unique and much more worthwhile. In this meeting Flow Theory was born. My further work on Flow Theory helped bring about a personal metamorphosis – a transformation that seems unstoppable.

Tuesday 1 November 1994

I spent a day writing down my new insights into the human dynamic under the heading 'Flow Theory'. I noticed others who have been thinking along similar lines, including John Heider (The Tao of Leadership) and Peter Senge (The Fifth Discipline). I enjoyed doing this. I sent Joe a copy.

Flash of the blindingly obvious no. 1: Flow Theory

People are complex, but Flow is simple.
Flow takes place all the time between people.

Flow is like water moving slowly and easily, finding its own path.
Flow is energy connecting one person willingly to another.

Some behaviours encourage Flow –
giving, offering, listening, asking, giving up, inviting, accepting, showing interest, facilitating, seeking permission, checking interest, respecting, honouring, trusting.

Some behaviours block Flow –
telling, taking, refusing, denying, manipulating, exploiting, ignoring, inflicting, imposing, forcing, tricking, ridiculing, withholding.

FLASH OF THE
BLINDINGLY OBVIOUS

Flow is reality unfolding through a true dialogue.
The experience of Flow is being accepted, valued, harmonious and blissful.

The effect of Flow is to open people out revealing deeper thoughts and feelings, inviting learning, change and growth.
Flow builds strong, trusting relationships.

Flow represents people moving forward together over time, like a river.
Either Flow exists or it is blocked; there is no partial flow.

Flow enables the highest levels of commitment, the best quality of work and the most outstanding corporate performance.

Wednesday 2 November 1994

Some thoughts on 'change' have been crystallizing recently as I sleep, walk and drive. I feel I need to express them.

Flash of the blindingly obvious no. 2: what is change?

Change is the source of all human progress and all human pain.

FLASH OF THE
BLINDINGLY OBVIOUS

In today's world there is vast structural change affecting everyone's lives. IT, new products, communications, media. New diseases, problems and insecurities. New opportunities and uses for people's talents. An education system that seems out of touch with the challenge of lifelong change and continuous learning, isolated from parental input leaving children with an incomplete, unbalanced view of life, which sets them up to face unnecessarily painful change later on.

Change imposes itself on us from the outside. Change can break people, growing from a small beginning to overwhelm their lives. Change can break relationships.

Change comes up from inside us, imposes itself on us and then onto others.

Change can be exciting and enthralling or it can be highly threatening.

A secure base in life can open people up to what is positive in change: learning, progress, improved lives. Lack of a secure base can plunge people down to the most negative and threatening side of change, producing compulsions, habits, addictions and pain.

Mostly change catches us unawares. I notice my response to change in subtle changes of mood: slight depression, anxiety, feeling empty, neutral, unmotivated, alone. These slight changes of mood are easy to miss but very important determinants of how I behave with others. Meditation reveals them to me.

Change can happen in a person in an instant: negative energy can be transformed into positive. A person threatened realizes they are secure. A person moves their attention from a depressing big picture to an immediate task. Humour takes something negative and eases tension through laughter.

Yin and Yang are thrown into opposition during change. The Yang (male, driving) seems to interfere with the Yin (female, accepting). In naive corporate change efforts Yang does not recognize that change is incomplete and ineffective without Yin. Yin energy must be engaged.

Friday 4 November 1994

Wrote down my old (flawed) and a new (improved, Flow Theory) paradigm of change.

Flash of the blindingly obvious no. 3: old and new paradigms

Here are five old mistaken assumptions:

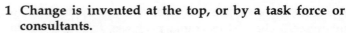

FLASH OF THE
BLINDINGLY OBVIOUS

1 Change is invented at the top, or by a task force or consultants.
   Mistake: Narrow ownership.
   Result: Change is first experienced by others as pre-determined and imposed.

2 Once the Board has communicated a proposed change, others will passively, trustingly and quickly accept.
   Mistake: Insufficient time to build commitment.
   Result: Change is driven and pushed on to others.

3 Change can be driven through a corporation by direct orders, carrots and sticks and more subtle, indirect forms of involvement – for example, facilitation.
   Mistake: Pushing/driving/manipulating builds and masks resistance.
   Result: Polarization into supporters and resisters, entrenchment, resistance.

4 Aligning the reward system produces commitment to change.
   Mistake: This drives resistance underground.
   Result: People pretend support. Meetings become like the Woody Allen film where the speech and the feelings subtext are disconnected and in opposition.

5 When change moves slowly the Board redoubles its efforts at driving change.
   Mistake: Fighting resistance with more of the same.
   Result: Resistance increases.

This old paradigm produces a workplace that is constraining, hostile and generates feelings of heaviness and threat. Everyone keeps themselves hidden and may experience others as guarded, devious or sub-human. Minds are closed to emerging priorities, possibilities and opportunities. The company underperforms.

Under a new paradigm:

1 **A charter of basic human rights and duties is in place to prevent the most inhumane and unreasonable behaviours giving people within companies the kind of basic human rights they enjoy in life outside such as the right to express your feelings, to be listened to, to information, to make decisions freely and so on.**

2 **The experience of work is fun and joyful.**

3 **The experience of leadership is uplifting, motivating and enhancing as opposed to debilitating, demotivating and degrading.**

4 **There are honest, committed and clear relationships between the corporation and the individual.**

5 **Superior performance arises from people deeply engaged and motivated by corporate goals.**

The company could benefit from the more wholesome workplace through:
• **costly resistance being visible and manageable**
• **reduced real change costs and lead times**
• **raised performance etc.**

Individuals could also benefit through:
• **reduced stress and insecurity**
• **clear information, realistic options, freedom of choice**
• **improved work relationships**
• **greater work satisfaction.**

CENTRAL LIFE QUESTIONS

Monday 7 November 1994

Today I feel positive, energized. I have just been reading a book that is currently topping the business books sales in the US, called The Celestine Prophecy by James Redfield (Warner Books, 1993).

What is so special about it? It is an adventure story set in Peru about the discovery of an ancient manuscript containing nine key insights into life. It contains material about energy and flow. Yes, it uses the word 'Flow' which I am very alert to.

The book triggered a search for my 'central life questions'. These spring from your father and mother. Your life is born between your mother's and father's truths. Your spiritual purpose is to take a higher perspective on what they stood for, to find a higher synthesis of what they both believed.

So what did my parents teach me? My mother taught me humanity, caring deeply for others, selflessness, but I also noticed that she was both exploited and criticized as naive. From my father I learned about a wider world, beyond family, of organizations, work, achievement, money-earning and discipline. I also learned the limitations of structures, the attractions and risks of moving to wild, unregulated, freedom.

Very different orientations. I find something in both. My life is about reconciling and transcending the problem they were unable to solve. For me, humanity is now the issue – finding a humanity that operates in the wider world outside the family, finding humanity that sustains both stability and freedom. Yes, that is getting close.

Tuesday 8 November 1994

Measurement team meeting. A great day and here is why: it is now 5.20pm and I feel full, positive, energized. I have felt like this most of the day. Inspired by the Celestine book, I decided before the meeting to be aware of energy: my own and the group's. I remembered my central life issues: humanity versus discipline and freedom, hard versus soft, organizations that are self-sustaining and people-sustaining.

During the meeting this awareness of energy had a very positive effect. It brought my attention outwards. Mid-morning I asked Rob about his new job and the opportunities it gave to enact the Deming principles. This really opened things out. Rob plunged into explaining something about variation to Sandra, expounding on the mistake of starting the corporate change programme before building a philosophical base. Sandra began describing her boss's mistake of too much push. I spoke about the blindness of change agents to their own behaviour. Rob said that he would want us to tell him if he had any interpersonal problems. I told him he had another problem: he pushed his ideas out without finding out where others had got to. His colleague from Scotland was nodding and agreeing.

I started talking about finding where the energy is and combining people's energy together. I talked about Flow, connection, the human dynamic, stating that Flow either exists or is blocked, that there is no in-between state. Rob brought us back to the safer ground of logic. It all seems to hinge on whether you rely on the power of logic or on the power of relationship. Maybe this is the soft and hard issue. The answer to my life questions is in this area. Logic has no power until the relationship/energy is properly in place, then logic has wings. (Shall I send Rob the paper on Flow?)

We then worked fast and easily. At lunchtime we went to a pub. Our conversation extended into some difficult areas of life, such as a tramp coming into church, a man waiting to jump off a London bridge, the stabbing of a 21-year-old in Woolworth's, Teddington. On the way back they were asking about me, my work, clients I work with, why I left PA. I admitted to feeling vulnerable. I felt fully engaged in the group. I felt full of energy, floating — and this without having drunk any alcohol.

The afternoon continued well. We made an action plan and had a meeting with our sponsors, made plans for a December meeting including a meal out. Finally Rob *suggested we should do some feedback at the next meeting to mark the end of our work together.*

Value through being aware of energy
Today's meeting had a special quality for me. I had decided to be aware of the interpersonal energies. This brought my attention outwards. We were all combining and flowing through drawing one another's attention outward. The contact between us felt more honest, truthful.

Wednesday 9 November 1994

Drove the kids to the childminder's and Helen to her Change Management course at Shell. Wrote down some insights on the limits to logic and power, triggered by discussions yesterday. I was very excited and energized by this. I sent it to Rob.

A meeting with Barry, who has acted as my professional mentor this year, in Hampstead. I took this opportunity to bring up my question about hard versus soft. Some interesting conclusions emerged.

- It is a leadership and management role to reconcile opposites.
- Management judgement is both a soft and a hard issue. The divide between soft and hard is artificially created. Already we do this with Thinking—Feeling, Sensing—Intuition.
- TQM (Total Quality Management) underlined how the 'soft' customer and employee issues create the 'hard' tangible business results.
- The BPR (Business Process Re-engineering) movement has failed. There was a false hope of eliminating the need for management judgement in the information age. The people side of BPR is the issue.
- The Zeitgeist fits this. We are rediscovering some of the awareness of the human dynamic that existed prior to the Thatcher/Reagan era.
- Now we are moving to a new point in the relationship

between people and organizations. A people value has come to the fore with customers and employees, but there is still denial of the changing contract, a myth of lifelong careers, and managers in the core are not trained to manage the non-core.

Flash of the blindingly obvious no. 4: the limits of logic and power

FLASH OF THE BLINDINGLY OBVIOUS

Logic and power are the predominant means of running organizations. When organizations face change, the limits of logic and power are quickly reached. A new method is needed to lead people united through change. Flow Theory is a new guiding principle to address this need.

First look at logic. Some problems are technical (hard) in nature, they obey the laws of physics, cause and effect, logic. A specific objective solution exists.

But the 'best, most logical' solution is often not found or not accepted. Why? Because technical problems involve people. People have an 'interest': the solution may make them become winners or losers. When feeling threatened by change, people are motivated to win in order to survive. Thus the human elements subtly begin to intrude in technical problem-solving. To tackle a technical problem without acknowledging the human relationship within which it is defined is to misunderstand the process.

Problems which are human in nature are inherently emotional, unpredictable and defy the laws of physics, mathematics or logic. What laws do they conform to?

They can be explained by Flow Theory. Flow cannot solve technical (hard) problems. Neither can logic solve human (soft) problems. Flow creates the human conditions for solving a technical problem; it provides the platform for logic.

So much for logic, what about power? Power is exercised continuously, but subtly, when people are together through implicit threats and rewards, even by such subtle means as drawing closer or moving away. The motive in exercising power is to gain a sense of control. The 'controller' gains in strength; the 'controlled person' feels weaker but experiences feelings of discomfort which block communication and feed a hidden motivation to get even. This can trigger bizarre behaviour after the event. Unequal power undermines teams and organizations.

Solutions to human problems arise from redefinitions and transformations within the relationship itself – shifting power, allowing the other a fuller sense of dignity and control. This transformation is the basis of Flow Theory.

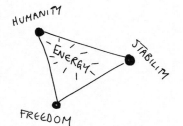

THE CENTRALITY OF
ENERGY

Thursday 10 November 1994

My life questions have led me into the work I am doing. I am finding that Change Management defines a domain in which the questions will get answered. Change Management exists in all human situations inside and outside work. Every situation calls for a balance of humanity, stability and freedom. In other words, hard and soft.

The Celestine book contains insights about energy that help me with my questions. Humanity is about giving energy to others. Stability is about being strong, centred and having energy. Freedom is about knowing your purpose, your path and having the energy to follow it. Energy is what sustains you. When I have energy I am free. I can gain energy from people around me provided the relationships are good. I also gain energy from stability and from freedom. So energy is something that transcends and enables a balancing of my three elements: humanity, stability and freedom.

I have a tendency to stay aloof, distant from people. Only by moving outside of aloofness do I gain the energy that makes me feel free, light, connected to the world outside.

Friday 11 November 1994

I was carrying a number of concerns today including:

- how to sustain the work and revenue stream
- adapting to Helen being on a two-week course
- the upheaval effect of reading the Celestine book
- a local planning enquiry
- the sale of our holiday cottage in Yorkshire
- my father's stroke

— and that's just for starters! Life is in flux and I'm in perpetual learning and re-evaluation. This is where this diary helps.

Lou Tice encourages the writing of affirmations (positive statements of intent) as a way of bringing direction to personal change. Today I wrote some new affirmations inspired by Celestine:

- I am keeping my energy high.
- I am appreciating the beauty of objects and people.
- I am observing energy.
- I am keeping my life questions in mind.
- I am aware of when I become aloof.
- I am discovering the messages others have for me.
- I am relating one-to-one with Tom and Georgia.

Monday 14 November 1994

Early this morning I woke up thinking about leadership (the Yang component of Flow??) and how it occurs.

A leadership example. We are selling our cottage in Haworth. Surrounding this we have all sorts of emotions. As we move closer to sale, we experience feelings of wanting to hold on. We expect to miss Haworth after it is sold. We expect to face questions of where to go in the holidays. But leadership in the matter of selling the Haworth cottage operates like this:

- We checked the state of energy of the stakeholders (family members affected).
- We found there was a lack of desire/energy to continue.
- Disposing of the cottage required energy/action – for example, briefing estate agents, solicitors.
- At certain rocky points, emotions about loss began to deflect us.
- At the rocky points we rechecked what we want to do.
- A positive outcome for all the stakeholders (for example, a holiday in Florida on the proceeds) helped to counterbalance the sense of loss.

Flash of the blindingly obvious no. 5: the nature of leadership

To lead is to extend your energy field outwards towards others.

Leadership is needed when people are lost, the route is unclear, there is danger or lack of time (in other words when you are up the creek without a paddle).

Leadership enables people to unite, to combine their energies.

Leadership is a natural part of change (but when does it overstep the mark, create resistance and impede rather than assist change?).

This leads to a definition of leadership which embraces soft and hard:

> **Leadership identifies where stakeholders' energy is, gives direction to focus the energy, helps create movement from status quo towards a more energizing position, rechecks, confirms, provides/ensures positive outcomes to maintain energy through the emotional ups and downs.**

FLASH OF THE BLINDINGLY OBVIOUS

Leadership breaks down when the leader's energy becomes disconnected from stakeholders. This can easily happen. Wrong leadership models encourage a breaking of the Flow – for example, a soft leader might find out where energy is with no idea of how or where to direct it.

If leaders do not interact with their people they lose interest.

If leaders do not appreciate their people they lose interest.

If leaders are not present, in Flow, energizing their people, there is no team, there is no partnership, there is no leadership.

When the leader is distant, then others reduce and/or remove their energy.

The leadership challenge is expressed in the change equation (vitality of vision plus dissatisfaction plus knowledge of first steps must be greater than the perceived costs for change to occur).

Tuesday 15 November 1994

Another leadership example. In 'The Wilderness', a conservation project involving parents and two local schools. Helen and I put a lot of energy 'out there' but we are not always patient enough to discover and focus others' energies. Until recently our leadership in The Wilderness has been egocentric, 'come on our terms or don't bother', holding power not sharing, not knowing where others' energies are. Others have been a little guarded/aloof towards us. Instead of finding a direction, I lazily allow individuals free choice which can block unison and progress and, by contrast, Helen pushes and rides roughshod.

The recent Wilderness meeting was different. Five

people assembled with Helen and me to discuss future plans:

- Helen summarized progress (but seemed a little cautious about changing anything).
- Others were bursting to put viewpoints and to suggest ways to proceed.
- One was very energetic, but quite 'jagged', isolated, hard to connect with.
- Another was milder, stronger and projected her energy outwards.
- A couple present were shy, connected together and making tentative interjections.
- Individuals were pushing energy out but not connecting well to each other.

I wanted to connect us all. The outcome contributed to by all of us was: 'the purpose is "educational" and to be specifically defined by using a questionnaire initially amongst the teaching staff'. To me, it felt good. Arising from the combined energies in the meeting, it had strength and integrity.

Wednesday 16th November 1994

Today my intention in our meeting was to keep Yin and Yang in balance. Keith entered with a bacon sandwich, a relaxed, easy smile and less tension. I mentioned our last meeting but he hardly seemed to remember it. I asked what role he wanted after the reorganization. He outlined three.

He spoke about a recent telephone session with an unusual female consultant in California. She told him he had problems in his energy field, he was plagued by self-doubt, a lack of vision and direction. She saw he had an idea, a technique, unique —one that was his own — waiting to be developed.

We spoke about 'being' versus 'doing': he wanted to move from 'doing' to 'being' but was afraid of losing creature comforts. An image came to me of a pendulum swinging. He referred to a fork in the road. Then I sketched him on a cliff labelled 'doing', ready to jump off into a space labelled 'being'. We worked with this for a while. Instead of trying to make a vision about the open space, he decided to reframe the cliff into a cloud or something – in other words, to evolve forwards his current role.

He gave me feedback: he felt lighter, had some steps defined, had something to get on with, he had gained value. I felt good, we had been in Flow, insights had come to us, we had created something that was grounded, real. We had both gained in energy. It was a change management dialogue. I had used Yin to engage the Flow and Yang to offer direction.

Keith expressed guilt about being self-indulgent. Was it boring for me? Shouldn't we have been talking about the department's business plan? I said no, there was energy in what we were doing, it was what we needed to do. Then I realized and shared my final insight: all of Keith's questions about doing versus being, around direction and vision, are resolved by becoming aware of his own energy and his moving towards what is more energizing.

Brilliant, just right! Keith understood and accepted. This conclusion also had great meaning for me. It answers all my questions. It provides the compass I need: read energy (my own and others) and then I will always have a clear direction. No more self-doubt or vacillation.

PROJECT PLAN	CLIENT: SEN. EXEC IN TELECOMMS COMPANY							
	MAY	JUN	JUL	AUG	SEP	OCT	NOV	DEC
1. First session – passive listening	✓							
2. Sent written feedback			✓					
3. Session to discuss feedback				✓				
4. Client postpones meeting					✓			
5. Commitment testing meeting						✓		
6. Spontaneous creative meeting							✓	
7. Doing, being + energy meeting								✓

EXTERNAL MENTOR PROJECT

Value through showing the client his direction

This meeting was the culmination of a coaching relationship extending over many months. It is not a well rounded success story. Rather, it involved much unrealized potential, slipping back and imbalance between corporate and personal aspects. In the end I was pleased with the final insight about the client needing to become aware of his own energy.

Sunday 20 November 1994

We visited a friend who is recovering from a quadruple heart bypass operation. He seemed thinner, fragile but he still has vitality and a sparkle in his eye. He will be off work until the New Year.

His operation was not just a shock to him but to all our friends. He had a pain, thought it was indigestion, it persisted, he went to the doctor and was rushed in for an operation.

He is 40. His wife is eight months pregnant. We have known him for more than 20 years. He was at university with us. It reminded me of our mortality. It underlines our advancing years. He has always enjoyed life. Recently he surprised us by saying, at 40, he was two-thirds the way through his life. The rest of us were thinking we were roughly halfway through. Then – just a few weeks later – this.

Value through experiencing a shock
This shock brings with it a change of view, a personal transformation, a review of life, a reconsideration of decisions that, until that point, have been fixed.

Tuesday 22 November 1994

I spent the day at York House, Twickenham attending a local planning inquiry. I was representing the local Residents' Association, fighting off an appeal by developers who want to build houses just the other side of our garden wall.

The most interesting part of the day was observing the two barristers. The barrister for the council looked 25 going on 50. He looked like Nigel Havers: slender face, pointed nose, slicked-back hair with a side parting. He was sharp as a knife, interrogating, making his point, acting, feigning hurt at the unreasonable behaviour of the other side.

By contrast the developers' team looked like a bunch of crooks. Their barrister had a moustache, a Savile Row suit that was just a little too tight for him, a smarmy, obsequious manner and a blunt, ineffective, improvised style. He looked unreal, a parody of a barrister — like a member of the Monty Python team.

If the developers win it can only be because the Planning Inspector is sorry for them. They seemed to make a mess of everything! The estate agent who claims he has been marketing the site for the last five years admitted under cross-examination that he had failed every test of good marketing!

Value through getting behind the facade

This experience reminded me of the strangeness, the formality, the role-playing, the banter, the charade, the facade that is part and parcel of everyday organizational life. Real, lasting change cannot occur in the facade unless you get behind it to the reality of people, feelings, values and beliefs. From there you can bring lasting change to the facade, but only change that is motivated from people's values.

Trying to get behind the facade to expose people's deeper motivation and then to ignore or exploit what you find is not only pointless, but damaging. It stirs up threat, self-protection, cynicism, resistance and confusion.

Wednesday 23 November 1994

I have two meetings today intended as 'Change Management Dialogues' — a new central activity for Page Consulting. They achieve client service, marketing, selling, product development all in one go. It is exciting. It brings me into a kind of partnership with clients and colleagues — puts us all on the same side of the table. Dialogues build relationships, generate value and produce work.

In my case, dialogues **are** the work: a joint exploration

GREEN GROCER | PAGE CONSULTING | SOLICITOR
FRUIT & VEG | DIALOGUES | • WILLS • PROBATE • CONVEYANC

A CENTRAL ACTIVITY

of the issues and the mystery in change. They process the change internally, moving through a personal change cycle to completion with feelings and behaviour reconnected in commitment.

Dialogues are valued and valuable to both parties. I gain satisfaction from them. They excite and energize me with the same heady feeling I sometimes experience from writing — big-headed, omnipotence welling up!

Thursday 24 November 1994

Last week I met a friend who works for BA. He was filled with enthusiasm after a leadership course in New Mexico — a high-energy week with lots of outdoor work using ropes, high-up poles, wires, jumping off a platform plus clapping hands, belly bumps and wandering in the desert. What did he learn from it?

- A leader gets more from people by pumping up the energy.
- A leader commits, does not sit on the fence.
- A leader provides more care and security for others than he feels he needs himself.

He regarded it as one of the better courses he has attended and felt it would be of professional interest to me; he is thinking of lending me the tapes and manuals.

The news broke last week of the closure of a company's site in the north of England with the consequent loss of around 300 jobs. Shortly afterwards an employee in Holland committed suicide. The grapevine explanation: he had moved from England to Holland the previous year, hated it, heard through internal communications that one company site was closing. Later an incorrect leaked press report had announced it was the Dutch site to close, so he built his hopes on being relocated back to the UK. With the announcement his hopes had been dashed and he took his life. This is all speculation: no one knows the true explanation.

Value through taking care with people
I had recently seen 'suicide' on a list of dysfunctional behaviours occurring during change but discounted the likelihood of this. This news underlined for me the extent to which our work in change management impacts on people's lives.

Friday 25 November 1994

We fixed a one-hour update meeting in Joe's office. It was not the time to discuss weighty issues. In this short time we rekindled the excitement in our work together.

He pointed to the cupboards that lined one wall of his office. The shelves were filled from floor to ceiling with books and folders on the subject of change management. Since taking up his new job he has painstakingly organized all this information.

The collection was impressive. So many writers – Hammer and Champy, Peters and Waterman, Nadler, Belbin, Beckhard, Fritz, Senge, Block, etc. Then there were all the consultancies: McKinsey, Price Waterhouse, EDS, Arthur D. Little, James Martin, PA, Arthur Andersen etc. It made our task seem daunting.

Did we know, had we read everything that was on the shelves? No. We had read much but not all of it. We

AN EMERGENT VIEW OF CHANGE

observed that all that already exists in a written-down form represented a kind of 'dominant paradigm' in change management. Did we agree with, and follow, all that these writers and leaders were advocating? No, but it was not all wrong. Our work represented an 'emerging paradigm' that was not embraced by what was on the shelves.

The shelves contained material that seemed dead, fixed, inaccessible, unreal. Change management to us was not about following a pat solution – a 'how to' manual, one right way. Instead it was about living, experiencing change, seeing what was emerging, understanding and learning from lived experience.

Value through an emergent view of change
This reconfirmed our earlier decision to write a diary – a diary was a real, lived, emergent phenomenon, not fixed, dead or programmatized. It was the other side of change management that is needed to understand and complement all the prescriptions and formulas already so well documented by others.

Monday 28 November 1994

SHEEP DIP TRAINING

Kinsley Lord is a name I keep coming across: old colleagues have joined them; Helen's course tutor was from there; Barry speaks well of them. I know them as one of the few firms that really understands change management. If we can pigeon-hole McKinsey as 'defining broad, strategic business requirements' then Kinsley Lord's point of difference is 'looking inside a company to leverage the capability to deliver'.

Their offices were in Queen Street backing onto St James Park, London. The CEO, an old colleague from PA, had agreed to an open-ended meeting with me.

Reviewing our early work with the healthcare company, the CEO said it was 'sheep-dip training' which his firm avoided like the plague! The approach was wasteful. Change is all about finding and building energy. Focusing change on to a needed business result is what connects individuals' energy into a change, making it important to them. Focus groups are used throughout an organization to develop vision at the same time as diagnosing where change energy is.

Getting the Board fully behind change is a question of courage. The Argyris method called 'undiscussables' has helped to open out Board discussion. Everyone prepares two lists in advance: what they think and what they plan to say. At the meeting people throw their lists away and talk through what they wrote.

Staff in a power station were galvanized by a threat from the chairman: they close if they do not become efficient. This was backed up by truth spoken by consultants: if they become efficient some jobs would disappear, if they did not all jobs would disappear. A voluntary redundancy assurance was in place. People began to work on change projects. Over a period of three years' continuous effort downtime improved from 17 to 6 weeks.

A 'light, fast re-engineering method' is saving millions of pounds at an oil refinery. The fees charged are a poor return for the value delivered. A consultancy fee cost is only a few thousands, but consultancies like Booz Allen are said to be charging £2 million for a similar process.

At Kinsley Lord they have a day every month when they all get together for development and learning. Recently they've had Mintzberg, Beckhard, David Maister, Gerry Johnson in as speakers at these meetings. Staff have a personal development budget to spend as they agree with their mentor. Impressive stuff.

Tuesday 29 November 1994

Earlier in the month I had started to think that leadership was the hard, Yang side of Flow. I now realize this was mistaken. There is a Yin and a Yang — a hard and a soft side — to leadership. I feel I know what these are. These are also the hard and soft sides of change management. In a sense, change management is bound up with leadership.

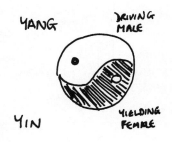

YANG
DRIVING MALE
YIN
YIELDING FEMALE

THE YIN AND YANG OF LEADERSHIP

**FLASH OF THE
BLINDINGLY OBVIOUS**

Flash of the blindingly obvious no. 6: the Yin and Yang of change management

Here is what I have realized so far about balancing Yin and Yang in my work:

YANG	YIN
Identifying threats and challenges	Reading energy
Stating needed directions	Building shared visions
Speaking harsh truth	Providing security guarantees
Confronting people	Supporting people
Advocating	Inquiring
Pushing people forward	Pulling, drawing people in
Generating a sense of urgency	Allowing time to decide
Designing the ship	Inviting people to come on board

Wednesday 30 November 1994

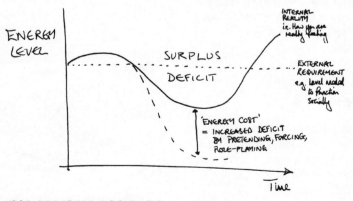

**THE 'ENERGY COST' OF
INAUTHENTIC BEHAVIOUR**

Driving to a meeting at the healthcare company at 8.00am I felt bad, gritty, negative. This was not a good position to consult from and, knowing I would not have time to meditate before the meeting, I decided to clear my mind by listing my current 'incompletions' on a yellow Post-It.

A long list of things were weighing me down, I felt briefly a sense of inadequacy, mortality and unworthiness, then remembered (from Loch Lomond) that this is a springboard for something more positive.

A little lighter in my mind, I moved on to consider the disconnect between behaviour and feelings. If I go into my meeting feeling terrible but pretending I'm happy then I have a massive energy leak. I need to recharge my energy, reconnect myself and focus or I become flat, passive and lifeless. A disconnect between feelings and behaviour is a source of weakness. Meditating, catharsis, breathing and the simple exercise of listing incompletions, are ways of reconnecting.

Flash of the blindingly obvious no. 7: change and energy

FLASH OF THE
BLINDINGLY OBVIOUS

Change requires energy.

The change equation (Beckhard and Harris) gives an approximation of the change energy available. It is a function of:

- dissatisfaction with status quo
- vision of a desired state worth aiming for
- feasibility, knowledge of first steps
- perceived costs of changing.

The change agent finds the change energy and the energy leaks.

Energy leaks exist in individuals (dissonance between feelings, values and behaviour) and in teams/ organizations (lack of alignment).

Energy leaks arise from incompletions such as broken promises, incomplete tasks, withheld communications, constant doing without reviewing and learning.

Plugging a leak involves surfacing feelings, identifying contradictions/disconnects/truth, allowing reconnection to happen through insight/vision/subconscious creativity.

Inner work is not enough. Usually external constraints also need to be challenged to close an energy leak.

SURFING THE WAVES
TOGETHER

Thursday 1 December 1994

The kids opening their Advent calendar argued and finally agreed who opens the first window to get the chocolate piece.

Joe said that, according to Richard and Brian, my consulting style had developed: 'Your communication channels are fully open, you are tuned to the people around you'. He said that, since our early work together in 1993, I have developed faster than he has. He now saw the value of a diary for reflection and learning.

We discussed how we facilitate. Joe previously operated as 'the guide who knows the path, the flora and fauna'. But his new team wanted something different: pure 'here and now' facilitation, 'a guide who simply helps them to see what is around them at any moment', real time, paperless, facilitator as equal rather than special person. This is the firing of synapses, the discovery of ideas and solutions in interaction with people. This is what Flow is: excitement, real-time interaction, sense of deep connection, huge value added, wind in the hair as you and the client surf the waves together.

We went on to express a new, visioning process that incorporated the human change dynamic. This felt exciting, innovative, inspired! Joe said that it had been a good meeting. I agreed. Then he rushed on to his next meeting at 12.30pm.

Value through putting our theory into words
Our discussion of facilitation represents us articulating a theory in use. Once articulated, instead of restricting how we facilitate, the theory of facilitation is free to evolve. This is what Argyris and McMaster seem to be saying.

Friday 2 December 1994

I arrived at the Chinese restaurant in Richmond 15 minutes late. The circle was formed. The energy was negative, separate, guarded.

There was open cynicism about the corporate change programme. Someone told about the recent closure of a factory in Lancashire: the Tina Turner theme tune we had used in so many conferences and courses was playing as the production line ground to a halt after its last run.

A flyer was passed round the table in which World AIDS Day was announced. Wherever the word 'AIDS' appeared it was replaced with the three-letter acronym of the corporate change programme. Someone asked the others to answer honestly the question: 'Has your career been enhanced as a result of the change programme?' Another said they would like to take a torch to the programme. Another said thank goodness the company made a major acquisition because it stopped them spending money on another change programme. There were stories of waste and lavish spending on hotels, parties and meals. This was the tone of it.

It seemed like a group of people coming to terms with failure. This group had been promised great things, then been pressured to produce, had surrendered themselves to the programme and had subsequently lost self-esteem rather than gained. Cynicism was the kick-back – the means of their recovering self-esteem and control.

The evening laboured on without really progressing. My contact with each individual was OK but the group did not gel collectively. There was no longer any reason to be together except to participate in a kind of wake. Yes, with hindsight, I believe this was the wake but was more English – sober and polite – than Irish – happy and drunken.

Value through waking up

Since writing this I am concerned that it is unbalanced and incomplete. The successes of the change programme have been huge. The company has woken up from a complacent slumber. There are new work methods and the beginnings of a common language that unite people from all parts of the organization.

Value through tangible measured gains
There was recently a set of awards in which workplace improvement teams calculated the tangible financial benefits delivered and expected from their projects. The benefits from the top 15 teams added up to $213 million. This is the tip of the tip of the iceberg: a further 99 teams entered the awards and their figures are not included and, of course, these 114 teams are a small subset of the total company-wide improvement activity.

Thursday 8 December 1994

I watched a TV programme about Machiavelli and his famous book, The Prince. Some top politicians referred to this as a primer – a basic introductory read when entering a political career. Machiavelli is Yang – driving, male, hard. You could say Margaret Thatcher was Machiavellian and fell only when she began ignoring his lessons about holding on to power. John Major is a nice chap and apparently less Machiavellian. But is he really?

The Prince is about 'ends', not 'means', and about maintaining power. There is little about integrity or authenticity. It is the antithesis of what we are proposing with win–win, partnership, teams and Flow. It is management by fear. It is command and control. It is manipulation. It is anti-empowerment. It sees the lowest in human nature. It sets up a 'dog eat dog; life's a jungle' paradigm. It presupposes scarcity of opportunity – there is not enough to go round, so fight for what there is. It is Theory X. It is the world of the deluded and paranoid director.

The Flow insight is about 'means' that create 'ends'. It presupposes abundance of opportunity. It is Theory Y. It is Yin – accepting, female, soft.

The two approaches do not fit easily together in business. Many business leaders favour the Machiavellian approach, but Flow is also needed to bring change, learning and real enduring strength to a business organization. Could Flow become a widely known and accepted 'way of doing business'?

Saturday 17 December 1994

Helen arranged tickets for the pantomime for around 30 people (parents and young children) followed by a gathering at our house afterwards. Like last year we asked Bob, our neighbour opposite, to dress as Santa. He was delighted. Same arrangements: parents bought a small present, wrapped and labelled for each child. I gathered the presents secretly in a black sack which I transferred to Bob. At 4.55pm Bob's partner Audrey came on some pretext to visit (but really wanting to watch Santa's performance). At 5pm Bob in full red and white garb knocked on our door and came in to distribute the presents.

What was different this year? The eldest children were a year older. They did not believe in Santa anymore. A gang of children were waiting in a bedroom upstairs looking out for Bob to leave his house opposite. Knowledge spreads fast through an informal network: the young children noticed and joined in. I tried to herd all the children back downstairs but it was impossible: it was like herding cats; they slipped through your legs.

When Audrey arrived there were knowing looks. Santa was able to go through the present-giving with relatively well-behaved children, perhaps afraid that trouble might mean no presents. The older ones lost interest and wandered off after getting their presents. One of the remaining children asked, 'Are you the real Santa?'. He said of course he was. 'How did you get here?' He said his reindeer landed in the park and asked if they had any oranges for the reindeer. This distracted them. Santa got away with it – at least with the younger ones.

Bob and Audrey are moving next month to the Isle of Wight. Bob has been Santa for the last three years. He started when Tom was four and Georgia only two. Each year there was wonder, magic surrounding his visit. We

WAKING UP TO THE TRUTH

have a photo of children gazing wide-eyed, their attention locked on to him. Bob improved his performance each time but each year the magic was dispersing a little. This year we just got away with it, but we will not do it again. Next year there will be no point: the children have lost their innocence.

Value through waking up (again!)
Is change a little like this – a sort of waking up to the truth, a passage from naive child to informed adult?

Friday 23 December 1994

It's cold, frosty and foggy outside. Someone outside the office window just slipped over on their bike as they were turning the corner. It is the last working day before Christmas. Helen is at home making final plans and preparations with Tom and Georgia.

Today I am finishing off work – clearing things up. I like the sense of completion before a new year starts. My project files for the year have all been tidied.

I am getting presents. Richard gave me a book called Energetic Meetings by Jeanie Marshall. The office is laden with cards. I've done a quick count. There are 44 cards in total. This makes me feel registered, in people's minds and in their lives.

At the end of an article I finished today I inserted lots of acknowledgements. I am pleased to acknowledge these people. They helped achieve the article. It was co-written with a client. I am involved in numerous change management dialogues.

I am no longer in a lonely struggle. I am amongst a group of people who are, in many different ways, supporting what I am doing. I am less on my own, less introspective and self-serving. My energy is moving outwards into the world, connecting with others. I feel good.

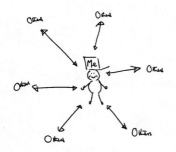

ENERGY CONNECTING WITH OTHERS

Saturday 31 December 1994

During the Christmas break I've been getting some thoughts on the nature of conflict and change management.

The notion of Flow we have used in developing the change management approach so far is more soft than hard. Last summer at the Tharpa course I realized that the front end of change management is all about conflict resolution. In other words, there are opposing interests and the change issue concerns how these are dealt with. This is hard not soft.

Change management is about keeping minds open, about removing threat and insecurity in order to bring people in to change. This requires facing truth, identifying people's real interests, making promises that you keep. To undertake these difficult tasks requires raising energy, building courage and confidence.

My previous tendency to avoid conflict was a weakness in change management practice which I have been tackling through my own personal development. I need to make sure this does not reflect itself either as a weakness or as an exaggeration in my future work.

I have started to realize what I want to do in 1995: I want to put **fire** into the work. On some level we are often holding back our real truth, avoiding conflict and protecting each other. But this is dangerous: it impacts on, and dilutes, the work.

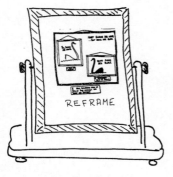

REFRAME

REFLECTIONS

Reflections on the reframe phase

What was really going on?
This was an unexpected rearrangement of my mental furniture. I was not driving this process. It felt very creative and exciting. It was happening semi-automatically. It emerged.

What is my theory about why?
Over the previous two years I had been challenging much of what I had learned about business life and about change management, going right back to my days with PA.

During this two-year period the diary method had helped me to see rather than deny reality by asking myself such simple questions as 'What is going on?' and 'How do I feel about it?'. I used the diary to explore my answers and find my truth. At the same time, I had been living with a dissonance between my previous anxious and inauthentic task-driven mode (thesis), and what I was learning through my various personal development activities (antithesis). I acknowledged the dissonance and the tensions. I lived with confusion and ambiguity for a time, allowing a gestation to occur.

The work with Joe and the change management project with Richard and Peter finally challenged me to express publicly what I thought change management was really all about. I was being encouraged to be authentic, true to my own beliefs and my own lived experience. I was challenged to make a 'synthesis' that encompassed both the old 'thesis' and my more recent experience of 'antithesis'. This was not easy.

Flow Theory and the other insights were the answer to these challenges. They were the harvest from the seeds sown in the earlier phases.

But Flow Theory was still very ethereal and disconnected from real life. The challenge in the next phase was to connect it to my work, to use it, test it, find what difference it made and fine-tune it to bring enhanced value.

EXERCISE: NEW SYNTHESIS

Work with a partner to practise reframing.

1 **Simple thesis. Make any simple factual statement that you believe to be true – for example 'Swans are white'.**

2 **Simple antithesis. Ask your partner to provide a simple opposing statement that is also true (the exception that proves the rule) – for example 'Some swans are black'.**

3 **Simple synthesis. Instead of debating thesis and antithesis, assume both to be true and working together, forge a simple statement that embraces both truths – for example 'Most swans are white, but some are black'.**

EXERCISE

4 Repeat the exercise, moving through steps 1, 2 and 3 with increasingly complex and emotional statements.

5 Discuss what you are learning about:

- your own behaviour patterns
- reframing
- transformation
- other learning.

Phase 5 Integrate

INTEGRATE

The fifth and final phase of the journey was living by a new belief system, continuously learning, facing pragmatic challenges and real difficulties and making some readjustments.

Sunday 1 January 1995

Spent New Year's Eve in a restaurant with 15 or so friends. Lots of wine. Some of us danced on the table at midnight. The dancing was unstoppable. The table broke. We entered 1995 with a bang, literally!

Wednesday 11 January 1995

I phoned Joe to find out how the big meeting had gone. He was very depressed. It had not gone well. The general managers were not engaged by the vision. They went along with it. They talked without listening. They pushed the vision back to Joe's team for further work.

Value through follow-up
The follow-up call showed care and interest towards the client: I was 'on the case'.

Challenged by resistance
An important high profile meeting, carefully designed and run by a highly experienced facilitator, was wrecked by the resistance of participants. Solution: bring all the stakeholders into the room, find out what really matters to them and facilitate an open dialogue.

Thursday 12 January 1995

I spoke to Joe again. His energy was restored: he was lively and energetic in his voice, his mind seemed alert, there was pace and animation. The difference was obvious. I found out that the meeting process we had developed was OK but our expectations surrounding it and the conditions under which it would work had not been properly set up.

Value through reading the client's energy
Noticing the client's changed energy signposted where to take the discussion.

THE DIARY

Challenged by ill-informed optimism
So far, our work on this project together had gone remarkably well. I had grown over optimistic. Solution: explore 'what ifs?', risks and obstacles at the planning stage.

Friday 13 January 1995

Good news! The management development programme we ran in a London local authority last year won a Department of Trade and Industry award.

Value through award-winning work
Awards boost client and consultant confidence to move further in search of value together.

Tuesday 17 January 1995

Rosemary and I discussed the 10 year(!) plan for Page Consulting using the Index of Change Energy to discover the obstacles. This was most informative. Rosemary said she often felt a bit like an outsider. My major block is to do with my communication with people around me – clients, contacts and colleagues, including Rosemary. We agreed on some positive actions to tackle these blocks.

AWARD-WINNING WORK

Wednesday 18 January 1995

Last night I had a phone call informing me that my father had a second 'bout of trouble' (euphemism for a stroke) affecting his left side.

Challenged by family troubles
I felt confused and emotionally blocked but also aware that how I acted over this news represented where my true (as opposed to espoused) values are. The temptation was to ignore and avoid an unpleasant situation.

Solution: before acting, reflect on what my values imply that I should do.

Thursday 26 January 1995

CHANGE MANAGEMENT
PRODUCT
DEVELOPMENT PROJECT

Meetings with re-engineering team re change management. Great progress. We identified 'stakeholders' and articulated their 'interests'. We discussed sponsorship and change energy. We built up the business case for change. We really started using the change management frame of reference and language. I could hear bells ringing. I could see light bulbs switching on!

Value through adopting a specialist language
Our use, in this meeting, of such terms as 'stakeholder', 'sponsor', 'interests', 'readiness' and so on enabled us to quickly reach the heart of the change issue. It also gave the participants access to a new way of thinking about change.

Thursday 1 February 1995

How did we get Richard's buy-in to the change management product? By helping him today with a real change issue he is facing. In the space of 30 minutes we elicited his 'business case for change'. We simply went through the four components of the business case:

- What is wrong with the situation now?
- What is your desired future state?
- What are your first steps?

- What are the costs and benefits of moving forward?

Two probing questions which made this powerful were 'What is really pissing you off?' and 'What do you really want to get/gain?'. These seemed to reach through to a strong, core motivation in the client. Richard went away empowered and energized. I felt good about this.

Value through connecting with client's motivation
The probing questions turned this from something academic to something real and engaging for the client.

Monday 6 February 1995

My brother and I visited my father in hospital. During the visit we had a conversation that would never have taken place except in these circumstances. We covered a number of practical matters but moved into real depth at certain points: good versus bad, God, what he learned years ago from my mother and so on. This was most memorable and unprecedented. Sobbing, hugging and 'thank yous' before leaving.

Value through speaking truth
We spoke the deepest truth we could speak together at that moment. It felt like the clearing of a log jam – the removal of some blockages that had built up over many years partly through blame and suppressed anger on my part, perhaps arising from parents' separation 20 years ago.

Thursday 9 February 1995

Awayday with top team of market research company to map out their journey into the future. Exciting opportunity to achieve deep engagement and trial the change management product.

The hardest thing was to manage expectations concerning the time it all takes in the face of pressure to

PROJECT PLAN

CLIENT: MARKET RESEARCH COMPANY

	JAN	FEB	MAR	APR	MAY	JUN	JUL
1. TELEPHONE BRIEFING							
2. CHANGE MGNT AWAYDAY							

push on to specifics such as role definitions.

When the meeting closed the energy was good, light, positive, liberated, realistic, aligned, ready to move forward and keen to complete on some things.

FACILITATING STRATEGIC AWAYDAYS PROJECT

Value through feedback

Here is some end-of-day feedback from participants:

- 'I have a much better understanding of where we all are. I found it liberating.'
- 'We started to build the trust and openness that we'll need.'
- 'There is a spirit of like-mindedness.'
- 'We seem committed to similar goals. This makes me excited and hopeful.'
- 'I have a better grasp of the issues in terms of company, people and goals.'

Value through experimentation

The best thing for me was experimenting with new methods:

- I explained Flow as 'sharing the oxygen in the room', tuning us into a 'feeling dimension' to the discussion, alongside the 'rational dimension'.
- I remembered to relax and maintain Flow. I found people using the term 'Flow'.
- I built in a step for participants to value themselves and value the others. This built a reserve of energy to tackle the difficult change issues they faced. In this generous climate my contribution was also valued.
- We followed the stages in a change management process and used the Index of Change Energy to uncover blocks.

- I flagged a moment when hackles were rising to build the team's awareness of conflict. I started to express a model for turning inherent conflict into unique strengths. This could be extremely important in my future work in the area of conflict.

Value through tangible results
A new management structure had been agreed. There was commitment to put it into use.

Friday 17 February 1995

Excerpt from my fax to a client in Australia:

> . . . now you explain, I can understand. What a wretched thing it is to be caught up in the forces of change.
>
> Work in change management is very exciting just now. It feels like a long awaited baby just being born. I have been learning for 39 years to produce what is now crystallizing!!! This story in some way connects my work and your current circumstances. . . .
>
> When Tom was a baby (yawn, don't parents go on!), his granddad in Bramley (the rhubarb-growing capital of Yorkshire) gave him a 3-inch stick of rhubarb. Tom was at the stage of grasping, holding but not being able to let go. As soon as he was given the stick he put it to his mouth. As soon as he tasted, he scowled (it was bitter-sweet) and moved it away from his mouth. A few seconds later he moved it back to his mouth again (had he forgotten the sourness or was he drawn again to the sweet component of the taste?) and the same cycle repeated for some time. Move it closer . . . move it away. Approach . . . avoid. Seek . . . hide. Attract . . . repel. Love . . . hate.
>
> In a way this pattern seems to go on through life for us all. We make small movements to and fro, we feel swells of emotion towards and away, but most of the

time we remain more or less in the same position. Only every now and then something moves us to some more decisive action such as leaving home, moving house, getting married, having kids, changing jobs (make your own list!).

Unfortunately when stirred into action we are poor at bringing others on board, doing the necessary explaining, influencing and reconnecting our needs with others around us. We end up frustrated at their lack of enthusiasm, pushing them, becoming desperate, making threats.

The people with power at the top of corporations have got used to pushing and threatening. People like you and me are on the receiving end. We learn to live with it, to adapt, to make a limited and calculated extension of commitment. We do not want to be like them. It feels wrong. They get backlash and inhibit the results they achieve. Is there a better way?

Yes. We are developing tools that help you to be proactive, decisive and to connect your motivation with others to bring about positive change. Put into top business leaders' hands the tools to give ways of introducing change that are less destructive. This translates into higher competitive and financial performance.

We're not there yet, but I think you can begin to see where my excitement is with this stuff.

In your shoes I would be using the Index of Change Energy first to align my
own motivation, then to work up a concise 'personal case for change'. You seem unhappy with what is going on around you. This is good. It is part of the fuel you need to move towards something that is even better for you. The dissatisfaction is there. Use it. Work on the future state that you do want to achieve. Envision your perfect future state. Start loosely with the

sensations you want to have. Don't worry that it is not real yet and has no substance. Allow the sensations to work on you over a period of time. Don't compromise anything initially. . . .

Wednesday 27 February 1995

Work with Peter has really moved the Navigating Change product on. The first draft is almost complete. Peter says he is now seeing the value from all of our previous discussions and meetings since September.

Value through gestation
It takes time and trouble to produce something worthwhile!

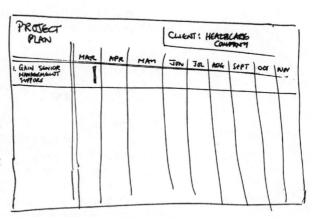

CHANGE MANAGEMENT PRODUCT DEVELOPMENT PROJECT

Wednesday 22 March 1995

Our sponsor e-mailed our facilitation course proposal to his boss in the US. We gained an immediate and enthusiastic response. We were asked to involve Garth as a consultant and also, if we wanted, to consult Peter Block. This was brilliant news! Peter Block had inspired me to write the article on being authentic in 1992. I could not believe that we might now be working with him.

FACILITATION COURSE DEVELOPMENT PROJECT

Value through winning senior-level support
Suddenly resources were being made available to our project.

DAY TRIP TO MUNICH

Wednesday 29 March 1995

Day trip to Munich to initiate a project. Flight delays, snow, closed runway, late arrival, challenged by the language, operating in a different business culture, setting off late for return flight, taxi crash and puncture, standing in the falling snow, rushing and catching the flight. Phew!

Monday 3 April 1995

To University of Warwick for AMED conference. I sat next to a publisher at dinner. He was looking for authors. I was looking for a publisher. I chatted with him about publishing a diary.

Value through uncovering interests
If we had not each revealed our interests to the other we would never have discovered a common interest in publishing this book.

Thursday 6 April 1995

After dinner Garth spent an hour with Len and me. Garth stressed that, in dealing with change, we need to account for addiction. Addiction has something to do with well trodden pathways in the brain – like well developed muscles they are easy to use, they are familiar. We also needed to recognize that change never occurs without pain. Pain is what propels you into a change situation. It is also what breaks an addiction.

PROJECT PLAN		MAR	APR	MAY	JUN	JUL	AUG	SEPT	OCT	NOV
CLIENT: HEALTHCARE COMPANY										
1. GAIN SENIOR MANAGEMENT SUPPORT		▮								
2. LATIMER MEETING TO DEVELOP PRODUCT			▯							

FACILITATION COURSE DEVELOPMENT PROJECT

Challenged by human nature

We seemed to be in deep waters. Developing facilitators is not simple! Solution: think more about addiction, pain and human nature.

Friday 7 April 1995

Here are some dilemmas I keep coming across:

Change is overdue and URGENT but . . .
    if I rush I SLOW it down.

I want the change to be PREDICTABLE but . . .
    when I try to use Project Management methods they
    prove UNRELIABLE.

I want to discover ONE WAY of handling change that
    works reliably but . . .
    every change situation requires a DIFFERENT WAY.

The harder I PUSH for what I want the more others
    RESIST.

I want to PERSUADE others of why and how to change
but . . .they only change when they DISCOVER why and
how for themselves.

We need EVERYONE to come on board but . . .
unless I allow CHOICE then people enlist grudgingly or
compliantly.

I want OTHERS to change but . . .
unless I change MYSELF they remain fixed.

Two of the central dilemmas seem to be:

- formal (task) versus informal (people) focus
- control versus letting go.

Monday 10 April 1995

Meeting with Bill, senior manager at a manufacturing
site. We discussed his organization as an example of a
self-organizing 'complex adaptive system' in which a few
simple rules, like genes, generate all the complexity and
variety of human behaviour. At Bill's site one of the
implicit rules is 'the leader knows best'.
    Other examples of 'complex adaptive systems' are:

- the food supply in any major capitalist city, such as
  New York
- the Internet WorldWide Web (not Compuserve which is
  centrally planned)
- driver behaviour on the M25.

For example, on the M25, estimates of usage proved
seriously wrong; an accident on one carriageway causes
delay on the other as drivers slow down to look. When
driver information is provided it influences behaviour (for
example 'accident at Junction 16' causes a proportion of
drivers to turn off, noticing this causes others to turn
off too and it is impossible to predict in advance what
proportions will stay on the motorway or turn off). If you

change anything, you do not know what will happen. Drivers are learning and adapting all the time. Outcomes are probabilistic and cannot be predetermined.

The rules are implicit, unconscious. When participants become aware of collective behaviour patterns (for instance, clusters and spaces between traffic on motorways), the rules are made visible, the probability of certain behaviours is altered and the whole population moves forward to a new stage of evolution. This is called a 'qualitative shift'.

Behaviour is like a 'life force'; it emerges spontaneously. Many corporations, in desperate straits, have attempted to interrupt the Flow, imposing change, forcing people to accept it by means of threats in order to survive and hold on to their jobs. Results in such programmes are often disappointing.

By contrast we were interested in 'change as a way of life': change is always happening, change is inherent in the continuous interaction between organism and environment. So how do you bring about change in an organization? You create conditions for a 'qualitative shift'. For example:

- Let go; trust the positives.
- Start by acknowledging people's capability and right to exist.
- Provide time and space for reflection.
- Share mental models, articulate and share the 'few simple rules'.

Value through sharing mental maps

This conversation went rapidly and easily. It arose from the combination of our views on change. Through the discussion we both made a 'qualitative shift' and advanced our understanding and practice.

Challenged by proving the value

My intuition tells me that this conversation was very valuable to us, both as individuals and to Bill's company. Unless we discover the dynamics of change all we do is repeat corporate history which is littered with failed attempts to change. But how can I prove this to sceptical business leaders? Solution: don't try to prove it; just discuss with them what, in their experience, works and what does not.

Wednesday 12 April 1995

It's Spring. I cycled with Tom and Georgia to drop them off at the childminder's for the day. The sun is shining. It is cool. The magnolias are shedding their blossom on the ground. I feel quite positive and optimistic. Helen has gone back to work after two weeks off with her broken foot. I have been thinking about addiction and pain.

FLASH OF THE BLINDINGLY OBVIOUS

Flash of the blindingly obvious no. 8: addiction

Homeostasis means the maintenance of equilibrium: there are small movements but, overall, the situation remains constant. An organism moves from its current state (resting) into a desired state (eating) back into the first state (resting). Homeostasis evolves/unfolds as an organism grows in relationship to its changing environment (for example, changing sleep requirements, different appetites and tastes in food).

Addiction is homeostasis that is frozen in its current form and is not unfolding. A junkie experiencing withdrawal symptoms takes a fix. The pattern repeats. Taking the fix relieves the felt need but also blunts the awareness of environment that leads to evolution.

Addiction is not just about drugs; it can occur in any behaviour pattern when that behaviour has become habitual (that is, routine, repetitive, without conscious control or full awareness).

Awareness is the key to recovery from addiction. When a behaviour pattern is visible and clearly dysfunctional (that is, against the survival interests of the organism), the organism spontaneously learns and changes the pattern. The presence of a drug that blunts awareness is a block to this.

Flash of the blindingly obvious no. 9: the pain of change

Change is natural and only painful if previous addiction has occurred – that is, previous awareness was blunted.

The pain is reduced if awareness can be extended progressively within a relationship of trust.

FLASH OF THE
BLINDINGLY OBVIOUS

Thursday 13 April 1995

Today a box arrived containing 22 pristine copies of Navigating Change.

I remember what was occupying my thoughts as I was waking up. It was an idea called 'moving the world'. It is a kind of metaphor for change energy and belief. It is an experiential exercise in which I make the following proposal:

We do not know how strong our belief is. We could move mountains but only if and when we realize the power that we already possess.

We could discover and demonstrate the power of our belief right here and now in this room. We could discover through making a physical change in the room the kind of change that we could bring about in our organization.

PROJECT PLAN		SEPT	OCT	NOV	DEC	JAN	FEB	MAR	APR	CLIENT: HEALTHCARE COMPANY
1. START-UP MEETING		▨								
2. VISION VALUES – WORKSHOP			1							
3. 1:1 MEETINGS WITH PETER				▨▨▨						
4. MEETINGS WITH TEAM							1 1			
5. RICHARD'S BUY-IN								1		
6. DRAFTING NAVIGATING CHANGE PROPER								▨▨		
7. DESIGN OF GRAPHICS + PRODUCTION									▨▨	

CHANGE MANAGEMENT PRODUCT DEVEOPMENT PROJECT

Look at the room. How do we feel about it? To what extent does it reflect our inner beliefs and values? What is present here that is inconsistent with our inner space? Let's spend 15 minutes making physical changes in the room to reflect our inner beliefs and values.

This 'moving the world' exercise takes only 15 minutes. It works if we are willing to participate. It does not cost a lot. It could be fun. Let's do it!

Value through recording insights
I'm slightly afraid that people might hang back but, equally, I'm excited at the potential of this 'moving the world' exercise. I think it will bond, unite, ignite and inspire a group and demonstrate the change that is possible. I might try it in a workshop or training course.

Thursday 20 April 1995

Checked in at hotel reception around 5.30pm. Splendid setting – my room overlooks the river.

At dinner I sat next to Ben, the US Vice President of the healthcare company who had called this meeting. A big idea came out of our conversation. Ben, like the Native Americans, sees the human being as part of nature not distinct from it. We all, as individuals, form part of the whole like the cells in a body. The whole sum of all the cells (humankind, animals, plants, environment, past and present) is the same thing as nature and the same thing as God.

The idea is unprovable but, as Ben put it, 'If you take it on board, how does it make you feel?'. The answer is that it makes me feel good, part of something larger, more significant. It gives me a place in the world. It shows me the importance of looking after myself so that I am fit, in good shape in both body and mind. It also shows me the importance of caring for others. It gives me a place in the community and the world. Wow!

I also talked with the company's Medical Director who has written a report on the 'Quality of Working Life'. The

Chief Executive and Chief Medical Officer started this when they were snowbound in a hotel together. In discussion they found that their quality of working life was low and their stress levels high. The report accepts that long-term stress inhibits the body's immune system and leads to serious diseases, such as cancer.

Challenged by mind-stretching conversations

At the time both the conversation about God and about the stress/immune system seemed rather 'way out', incredible, unusual and inappropriate for a business meeting, but I suspended my judgement. I now see that they are relevant issues for individuals who are assessing their relationship to corporate life. Conclusion: beware of making hard and fast rules about what is appropriate or inappropriate in business.

Friday 21 April 1995

We started the dialogue group at 8.30am – about 10 of us in a circle. Garth and Ben made an introduction. People took turns to talk and also wrote on flipcharts to make a kind of record. The conversation turned naturally to the individual and the organization and we became deeply immersed until our break around 11am.

Afterwards it was not easy for us to get back into the subject. We dabbled on the surface. Later someone had a head-on clash with Bill who wanted to hold a completely open-ended dialogue to see what would emerge. The other person wanted rules and structure. The group helped sort them out.

Significant ideas that I gained from the meeting were:

- Papiermaché layering of knowledge on to people is not learning, but smothering.
- Learning is digesting the layers imposed from outside like a chick breaking out of an egg.
- Parenting and schooling is where it all starts.
- Change happens in a situation of fluidity within active, vital relationships.

Challenged by dialogue meeting

I am so excited that this meeting took place. It is a network forming. But, at the same time, I noticed that not everyone felt like this. There was scepticism about the value. There was guilt at spending company time and money on it. How could we prove its value? Resolution: express a pragmatic business case for dialogue.

Wednesday 3 May 1995

As I changed trains at Clapham Junction, I hovered in the crowd at the top of the steps waiting to see whether the next train to Victoria would be at platform 12 or 14. I noticed how one person moving downwards on the other side of a crowd of 30–40 people causes the whole crowd to move down the steps to meet the next train on platform 12. It was as if we were one being, moving together. All our senses were linked – there was a rapid communication between all the senses and all the limbs. We all moved together.

I attended a course with Joe. During the exercises I produced an embryonic proposition for Page Consulting: 'generative change through a generative relationship'. Joe preferred quite a different one: 'thought leader working with other thought leaders'. These both begin to define, in shorthand form, a domain within which Page Consulting operates. These extend beyond 'change management' and specifically address the creative, generative element of change rather than the cost-cutting BPR (business process re-engineering) strand. They are post-BPR propositions.

Challenged by articulating a business proposition

I wanted to find words to express to clients the business value that is delivered by my work. Solution: draft one and discuss it with a client.

Monday 15 May 1995

Swallow Hotel: free-form meeting, no formal agenda, seeing what emerges. Discussing how to format a series of one-day workshops for management teams in each European country, Joe wanted to give instruction on change management before a diagnostic exercise. I was uncomfortable with this, and an insight emerged:

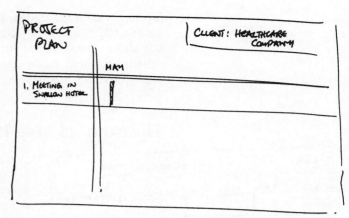

MANAGING CHANGE IN EUROPE PROJECT

- all change is about relationships
- no relationship = no change.

When I said this to Joe, he looked incredulous at first but then he accepted that what I said had a ring of truth. He said it was a troubling concept. He did not necessarily want to be in a relationship with his clients.

Challenged by discovering differences

Finding out that we were operating from different assumptions about the person-to-corporation relationship made me uncomfortable. Solution: share assumptions.

Tuesday 23 May 1995

My 40th birthday and the last day of our holiday. We spent the morning at our hotel in Spain and on the beach.

Later, back at home, we talked about what I wanted over the next five or so years. I did not want much. I want good, interesting and engaging relationships with all those around me (that is, Helen, Tom, Georgia, rest of family, neighbours, friends, work colleagues). Not necessarily continuously deep and intense relationships but with positive effects arising from them. I wanted others around us to experience the prosperity and success we are now experiencing.

Thursday 25 May 1995

Set off for Latimer Mews at around 7.45am. Another beautiful sunny day. Len, a healthcare company client, and I discussed organization changes, including the departure of our sponsor's two bosses and their replacement by one new person with a reputation for a hands-on, pragmatic, business-driven approach.

FACILITATION COURSE DEVELOPMENT PROJECT

Challenged by changing context

The change of sponsor's boss was bad news. We had enthusiastic commitment from the previous people. The new boss might not agree even with continuing the project. Solution: rush and complete our prototype course before the new person stops the project!

Tuesday 30 May 1995

Georgia came in beaming, with chocolate round her mouth, and presented me with an envelope labelled 'Georgia's tooth'. Her energy and lack of self-consciousness is so endearing. She tells me how she twisted and pulled it out. The tooth fairy box is ready.

Helen told me her sister is suffering from an eye problem. We talked about the long list of problems in her sister's life.

Thursday 1 June 1995

Quite a day for us. Two pieces of big news:

1 Helen has been offered her voluntary severance from Shell. She gets a tax-free lump sum and leaves at the end of July. She is looking forward to a pleasant summer with the kids.
2 I met the publisher. We agreed terms. We have to deliver the manuscript by the end of December 1995.
Helen and I shared a bottle of Moët, a gift left over from my 40th. There was a contented positive atmosphere.

Friday 9 June 1995

Helen's sister was taken to hospital today with a suspected stroke.

Saturday 10 June 1995

It is not a stroke but a brain tumour. The outlook is not good.

Sunday 11 June 1995

Rainy Sunday. Cycle practice. Our last proper practice before the London to Brighton ride next Sunday. We rode 18.8 miles round Claygate, Oxshott, Esher and back via Hampton Court and Bushy Park.

I asked Helen to read some sample diary entries for the book. She said it was brilliant. She was happy with what I had said. She suggested that I ask the kids to do some illustrations and include some of my own scribbles and sketches.

Wednesday 14 June 1995

PROJECT
PLAN   CLIENT: MANAGEMENT CONSULTANCY FIRM

	MAY	JUN	JUL	AUG
1. BRIEFING				
2. RUN 3 DAY COURSE				
3. FOLLOW-UP MEETING				

CONSULTANT DEVELOPMENT PROJECT

Last day of a course for management consultants. They were keen to learn more about resistance. Then, in the first exercise, which is normally easy (agree the five key qualities of a consultant), we triggered huge resistance. Participants were gathered round a table clustering yellow Post-Its, trying to reach consensus. They were becoming bogged down in debate, not listening to one another, not trusting that others had anything of value to say, treating the exercise as a personal crusade for 'rightness' against the group's wrong view.

I called 'time out' and asked the group what was happening. The two dominant members leapt blindly back into debate. I stopped them again and asked the others to comment in turn. Then the group tried once more to reach a decision. This time it was better – they decided to vote but the decision reached was ambiguous, not supported by the whole group, and argument broke out again!

We gained a powerful experience of resistance and conflict but I wanted more time to develop and complete the learning.

Challenged by egocentric, intelligent people

Debate was at the level of 'me right/you wrong'. The group was prone to divide and fight instead of including and building on diverse views. I am beginning to realize that everything worthwhile and enduring in this world occurs through a willing combination of human talents and energies rather than through some clever ego-driven exploitation. Solution: raise 'here and now' awareness with conflict styles inventories and 'time outs' until those who are blind start to see.

Thursday 15 June 1995

Meeting with Joe and Bill. Both are experimenting with enquiring/pull/Yin styles, restraining themselves from driving/pushing. They are experiencing benefits, seeing the client fill the vacuum they create.

After lunch Joe and I started to develop a powerful diagnostic workshop that unearths 'what is real'. We discovered that a series of 'why' questions triggers defensiveness, self-loathing, a downward-closing spiral, causing participants to shut off. We want to engage positive energy, triggering an upward-opening spiral in which new change possibilities are embraced. This requires an unconditional loving – a caring. We found that asking 'what really matters?' instead of 'why, why?', and aiming to define 'central life questions' is the way to proceed.

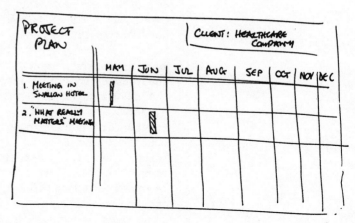

MANAGING CHANGE IN EUROPE PROJECT

Challenged by anxiety for a result

I felt anxious. We were without an agenda doing a free-form dialogue. I felt uncertain about whether we would produce a result that would justify my fee. We shared previous insights and generated new ones, covering the complex terrain of personal and organizational change. Solution: make expectations explicit without imposing a constraining structure. Articulate how such sessions produce value for the client.

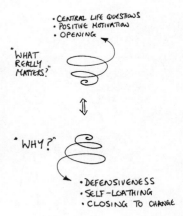

Monday 19 June 1995

Meeting with Barry and the Medical Director from the healthcare company. We discussed business

ENGAGING POSITIVE ENERGY

---

transformations. A computer mainframe company employed a few professional services people in support roles. When the business was redefined from 'selling hardware' to 'selling solutions' the company turned itself inside out. Support people became consultants at the leading edge, in charge of the customer relationship and the revenue stream. The new consultancy soon overtook the mainframe business and demanded independence from it.

A similar transformation may occur in healthcare with a move from an 'illness, pharmaceutical' business to a 'wellness, life style, diagnostics, solutions' business. New competencies will need to be grown, both within and beyond the existing (R&D, manufacturing and selling) competencies to make the transformation.

I realized that a business transformation is a 'reframing' that depends upon many individuals being able to 'reframe' their own contributions. This is not easy.

Wednesday 21 June 1995

I walked back from the childminder with Tom and Georgia. With me I brought two peaches, two muesli bars plus a tennis ball to throw. I was able to create a few 'happiness-producing moments'.

Sunday 25 June 1995

Georgia said something that touched me – 'Daddy we haven't seen your happy face today' – and she looked deeply into my face until I smiled. My mood did change: I became happy.

Thursday 29 June 1995

Awayday with the partners of a market research

CHANGING MY MOOD

company to develop ten-year vision plus three-year and one-year development plans.

We started by discussing vision as 'emergent', not something mechanistic. We sought to create the conditions for emergence: listening, finding personal motivation, combining into a corporate vision. I led a visualization exercise on 'what really matters to you as a person' to get us started. After this we walked outside on the lawn in the sunshine. The energy was positive. I felt a gentle openness in the others. We then shared and combined what they had produced, finding some shared corporate themes. One memorable theme was 'to be a company with soul'.

After this 'head-in-the-clouds' directional stuff, it was time to get real, anchoring each of the visionary themes in harsh current reality and making specific plans to move forward.

When we closed I felt very happy and relaxed. I stayed behind with two of the others, sitting in the sun and chatting over a beer.

Value through engaging positive energy
This day brought together a lot of my learning over the last couple of years. Something did seem to emerge today – something real, connected deeply in individual motivation, something shared and strong.

Monday 3 July 1995

I drove in the afternoon sunshine to set up the facilitation course. The course was to be experimental – a prototype – pushing beyond the normal limits and helping to produce a robust but creative course design. We wanted a room set up as a formal 'Work Place' with

PROJECT PLAN — CLIENT: MARKET RESEARCH COMPANY

	JAN	FEB	MAR	APR	MAY	JUN	JUL
1. TELEPHONE BRIEFING	▨						
2. CHANGE MGNT AWAYDAY		▨					
3. 10 YEAR / 3 YEAR / 1 YEAR PLANNING						▨	

FACILITATING STRATEGIC AWAYDAYS PROJECT

PROJECT PLAN — CLIENT: HEALTHCARE COMPANY

	MAR	APR	MAY	JUN	JUL	AUG	SEPT	OCT	NOV/DEC
1. GAIN SENIOR MANAGEMENT SUPPORT	▮								
2. 'LATINER MEETING' TO DEVELOP PRODUCT	▪	▮ ▮	▮	▮ ▮					
3. DISCUSSION OF ORGANISATION CHANGES			▮						
4. UK BASED PROTOTYPE					▨				
5. US BASED PROTOTYPE						▨			
6. DEVELOP PRODUCT TO PILOT STAGE + TEST							▨		
7. COMPLETE FINAL PRODUCT + ISSUE									▨

FACILITATION COURSE DEVELOPMENT PROJECT

phones, desks, fax machines etc. The other room was to be a 'Learning Room' with a circle of chairs, a flipchart by each chair, tables full of visual, auditory, kinaesthetic and miscellaneous learning resources. The hotel management was confused.

Len said, 'Stop walking around like that – you're making me anxious.' I was anxious myself. Eventually the rooms and equipment came together and I did relax.

Tuesday 4 July 1995

There were only five instead of the intended 12 participants (a disappointment for us all). With the current uncertainty about jobs, people feel safer sitting at their desks.

We led the group to the 'Work Place' and kicked off the course. It felt good. Then we moved into the 'Learning Room'. Ambient, light, airy music was playing and the video camera was running, filming people as they entered. Some time was spent explaining the room layout and starting to play with the many facilitation resources. The mood was light, fun.

After a full day of awareness and skill extension exercises, we took feedback from the group and learned that they valued this unusual opportunity for development. They would not be offered it in many companies.

Wednesday 5 July 1995

We moved between the 'Learning Room' (for awareness-raising/skill-building) and the 'Work Place' (for needs identification, trying things out and application planning). There was practice, feedback, use of video. We worked primarily on energy, conflict and interventions.

We had a delicious Mexican themed dinner and a hat-making contest **but** I had my first sense of discomfort — there was a tension in the air.

Thursday 6 July 1995

We thought the prototype was proving OK: participants were learning but we knew some changes were needed. In the final feedback session, we asked if the course development should move ahead. The answer was no, not in its present form but yes, with the changes identified in the feedback. We exchanged gifts of wine, 'thank yous' and books.

As I was leaving, our sponsor called me over to tell me that the course planned in the US for August was cancelled; the style of the course was wrong, and fundamental rework was needed.

CLIENT: HEALTHCARE COMPANY

PROJECT ON HOLD

1. GAIN SENIOR MANAGEMENT SUPPORT
2. INITIAL MEETING TO DEVELOP PROJECT
3. DISCUSSION OF ORGANISATION CHANGES
4. UK BASED PROTOTYPE
5. US BASED PROTOTYPE
6. DEVELOP PRODUCT TO PILOT STAGE + TEST
7. COMPLETE FINAL PRODUCT + ISSUE

MAR | JUN | JUL | AUG | SEPT | OCT | NOV/DEC

FACILITATION COURSE DEVELOPMENT PROJECT

Challenged by failure

This was a blow. I felt the experimental nature of the prototype had been misunderstood. We knew how to tighten the product. We had committed to offering the US trainers an opportunity to beome involved at the formative stage but we were not to be allowed to do so. We were exposed with this course, lacking solid senior-level support. The mood of the times had changed: our course needed to be harder, business-oriented, delivering direct bottom-line benefits. However we rationalized it, we had failed. It was unclear how to move forward. Conclusion: make sure you have solid senior-level support before attempting anything experimental or exploratory.

I'M MISUNDERSTOOD. WE'VE MISJUDGED IT. WE'VE FAILED

CHALLENGED BY FAILURE

Monday 10 July 1995

Greenpeace protesters (against the French plans to resume underwater nuclear testing) were removed from the Rainbow Warrior. New Zealand, Australia, Germany and other governments plus, of course, the inhabitants of nearby islands are outraged both at the plans and at the treatment of protesters.

Challenged by world events
I felt a sense of deep injustice, a violation of basic human rights; a government operating by 19th century imperialist standards, misjudging the mood of the times. Solution: ?

LIFE CHANGING DEVELOPMENT PROJECT

Tuesday 11 July 1995

A training day with a consultancy called Knowledge Based Development. We were asked to state a problem or issue we faced. I outlined my dilemma in change management between generation one (simple, traditional, business-driven, cost-cutting, desperate) and generation two (generative, emergent, enlightened, leading-edge etc).

Value through a new perspective

We were encouraged to look at life as a series of conversations. We covered much ground on speaking and listening. We learned about different modes of listening (for example, listening for meaning, for motivation, for direction, for possibilities and so on) and speaking. This way of thinking opened up new possibilities for me.

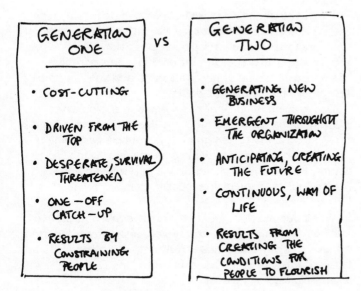

TWO OPPOSING PARADIGMS IN CHANGE MANAGEMENT

Value through powerful, motivated stance

Shelly, our trainer, was filled with energy. She was speaking from her core, not working from notes/manuals. She was using anecdotes, sharing herself with us, being totally present.

Thursday 13 July 1995

Helen's last day of work. Leaving party on 10th floor at Shell Mex House. We spilled out onto the balcony overlooking the bend in the river. London was at our feet. I took Tom and Georgia on the train. Nice posh evening. Helen made an entertaining (and moving) speech recalling ten years of people and changes.

The work diary has gone from full to empty. There are a few opportunities — mostly small. Maybe that is all I need while I am writing the book. Luckily we've built up some reserves of cash.

I thought about what we learned the other day from Shelly: attend to the 'background' and things emerge in the 'foreground'. The background conditions for business are: trust, track record, relationships, partnerships, win–win, expression of need, interest and yes, I'm coming to something — 'declaration'.

Declaration, said Shelly, is a 'speech action' that distinguishes leaders. JFK did it, Martin Luther King did it, the US Constitution does it. It involves becoming a mouthpiece, to express what others want, what life wants, to go beyond the evidence and make a bold directional statement like 'putting a man on the moon' or 'I have a dream'.

What Declaration would I make? It could be tied in with the book which is about expression, about freedom and about integrity in business. Authenticity came close but it is a righteous position, laden with 'shoulds'. So 'expression' comes closer.

Flash of the blindingly obvious no. 10: freedom of expression

FLASH OF THE BLINDINGLY OBVIOUS

I stand for 'expression' as a step towards a deep, strong connection of energies. This is a basic human freedom often denied (or surrendered) in business at great cost to everyone. In rare hotels the smile on a waitress's face tells a different story. Also we hear this about Body Shop, Ben and Jerry's, Virgin Airways and few other businesses. Such businesses are strong, and they represent the future.

The freedom is two-sided: giving freedom to others (including customers) and demanding the freedom for oneself.

The book will be an example of freedom of expression, an invitation to others to express themselves and a demonstration of how much there is to be expressed. It is a kind of awakening, a bringing to life, a stirring of consciousness.

Friday 14 July 1995

After a mid-year review this is how I see my current position:

- I am in the middle of change.
- I live on the edge, risking a little, failing a little, generating powerful learnings.
- I am finding my way.
- My direction is towards integration, integrity.

I spent some time putting together a draft Declaration.

A Declaration

MY PRACTICE helps clients (people, teams and organizations) to survive, develop strength and become 'generative' by finding what is real, solid, centred and motivated in their lives.

I DO this by directed exploratory discussions (explore, express, declare) which help the client to articulate their current 'theory in use'. Once this is expressed, learning, change and evolution can happen spontaneously and easily.

I REPRESENT my practice because I am surviving, developing, strong and centred in myself while listening FOR the client.

I USE various techniques including visualization/meditation, mind-mapping, provocative ideas/theories, appreciative inquiry, interpersonal feedback, exploring conflict/dissonance, listing incompletions (to restore control) and facing failures (to generate rich learning).

I MEASURE results by capturing at the outset the client's intended results (both in a broad sense and specifically from the sessions) then conducting review discussions from time to time.

I RECOGNIZE that results (monetary profit, visions, leadership and so on) are 'emergent phenomena', so I work on the 'background' from which results emerge as 'foreground'.

I DO NOT ever know where the work will lead in terms of specific results, but I do know that it quickly produces very powerful learning, releases energy, enhances opportunities and leads to higher performance.

I BELIEVE that this work offers huge value to individuals, to groups and to organizations, and I am keen to assist organizations with developing their own competence in these methods.

Wednesday 25 July 1995

A workshop at the local library, run by the borough. All locals welcome. We walked round the village in the sunshine: along our road, through the park, into the church, down to the bridge, back along the high street etc. We were asked to look for what was interesting, what we want to preserve and what is an eyesore. Councillors and council officers were there.

Later we were given a chance to express our views and wishes, which will be written up into a conservation area study — a positive, proactive opportunity to influence the future of the village. Great. Let this end the years of erosion and compromise.

Value through a shared journey

Why not do this in companies? Divide up into mixed groups, include all levels, all functions, all stakeholders and just walk round looking for what is good and what is an eyesore. Then devise a way of pooling views to achieve a consensus.

Tuesday 8 August 1995

Spent the morning at the rocky stream near Grasmere moving rocks to make deep pools. As we were leaving in the car, Georgia said to Tom, 'Do you like me?' Tom replied, 'Sometimes.' Georgia then asked, 'Do you like me now?' Tom said, 'Yes.' Georgia asked, 'Did you like me at the rock pools?' Tom answered, 'Yes.'

Watched a TV programme about Trevor Baylis, an inventor living on Eel Pie Island who, while listening to a programme about Africa, came up with the idea of a clockwork radio which did not need batteries. He then faced a long hard road to convert the idea into a commercial product despite the clear need for it. Big firms ignored his letter. BBC's Tomorrow's World got him started, and, within a year, a factory of disabled people was producing them in South Africa. The inventor went out there and wept when he saw the factory. Later he was photographed with President Nelson Mandela.

Challenged by lack of support
I was struck by how difficult it was to bring this important idea into reality. Now it has been given life it is changing people's lives. Solution: persevere.

Wednesday 9 August 1995

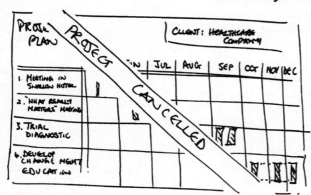

Joe is back from his holiday. He said I deserved an explanation for the change of direction on the project. He needed a solid old-style change management product to bring his three-person team together.

MANAGING CHANGE IN
EUROPE PROJECT

Challenged by expressing a complex set of ideas
Joe said that we still need to develop new-style change management, but the problem is we cannot describe it yet. This makes us vulnerable and blocks our progress. Solution: it's a matter of trial and error. Keep refining and testing. Express the tangible value that comes from the new ideas.

Wednesday 16 August 1995

As I lay in bed I thought about my positioning as a consultant. One client wants to be 20 miles ahead of everyone, be leading-edge, building a team of advanced specialists. I am happier about two miles in front, helping others to advance.

Monday 21 August 1995

Extract from a letter to a client in Australia:

. . . it's proving to be a strange summer for us. We had planned to go to Florida with Helen's family, but we had to postpone it as Helen's sister is very ill – she has a brain tumour. As you can imagine, this is very worrying.

Then two projects were postponed, one of which would have involved a trip to the US. So I've more time on my hands than I can remember. Helen left Shell at the end of July with a voluntary severance cheque: I'm not the only one who has time free.

This new sense of the abundance of time was good at first. But quickly the pleasure was replaced by a sort of empty feeling. Last weekend I did not want to do anything. Helen, Tom and Georgia had the same 'bug'. Helen said it is a symbiotic relationship. I am surprised at the extent of our interdependence. Anyway we seem to be moving again now.

You may have heard it is our hottest summer for over 200 years! We are becoming like Europeans (or Aussies?) wearing shorts every day. We walk on the shady side of the street and hide indoors until it is cool enough to go outside in the evening.

Last night we invited friends round for a barbeque. We used the dining room table in the garden, with a white tablecloth. It was a pleasant picture. We sat there drinking and eating until around 9pm. Tom lit candles for us. The air was still enough to let them burn for some time. Georgia was splashing in the paddling pool in the dark, then wrapping up in a towel and giggling.

Thursday 24 August 1995

Day with Knowledge Based Development in gothic-style hotel on the banks of the Thames. Rob, the trainer, asked what had occurred since our last session. I said I had spent the summer in the neutral zone. I was interested to reconnect with my value as a consultant, particularly the value I add to the corporation rather than to the client as a person.

Rob asked me what I really cared about. I said getting my talents used in the world, passing on what I have learned. He helped destroy the generation one (that is, what you can do but don't want to) versus generation two (what you want to but can't) divide. He saw my work as concerning the transformation of people and organizations. He suggested 'Leaders of Change' as a description of Joe's and my mission — leaders in the sense of showing others by going first. He said I was to stop being Mr Helpful and to think of myself a little more!

PROJECT: LIFE CHANGING DEVELOPMENT – R&D
CLIENT: HEALTHCARE COMPANY (ME)

Task	1993 OCT	NOV	DEC	1994 JAN	FEB	MAR	APR	MAY	JUN	JUL	AUG	SEP	OCT	N	D	1995 J	F	M	A	M	J	J	A	S	O	N	D
1. BRIEFING	▮																										
2. ACCELERATED LEARNING COURSE		▮																									
3. MANSFIELD LEARNING COURSE			▮		▮	▮		▮						▮			▮			▮	▮				▮ ▮		
4. AMED TRANS. DEVELOPMENT			▮																								
5. AMED – CLIENT RELATIONSHIPS					▮																						
6. AMED – TRANSITION						▮																					
7. WRITE & PRESENT REPORT				▨▨▨																							
8. PERSONAL DEVELOPMENT METHOD							▮																				
9. AMED – CHALLENGING ASSUMPTIONS							▮																				
10. THARPALAND COURSE									▮																		
11. FACILITATOR DEVELOPMENT COURSE											▮																
12. KNOWLEDGE BASED DEVELOPMENT																								▮ ▮		

LIFE CHANGING DEVELOPMENT PROJECT

Value through having something at stake

Rob said that finding what really matters to the client – something they care deeply about – is all that counts, the rest is detail. It might not necessarily be about their work but it usually is. Commitment must be tested. They should be given a choice to take action if they care, not to if they don't – but to be clear. Then you define a simple project in which they put this something at stake, and you block all the back doors!

What I put at stake was defining how value gets created through my work.

Friday 25 August 1995

Up early to Maidstone to meet a colleague in his oasthouse office. It is close to where my mother used to be a country GP when I was a small boy. I became melancholy; the mists had come down, were swirling, transporting me in time. I remembered being in the car as a small boy with my brothers and sister, sitting outside houses during my mother's rounds, playing with the handbrake. I cared. I felt my heart ache for those old times. I remembered my mother's selfless caring. I remembered her loneliness and the neglect she experienced.

Friday 1 September 1995

Following the course with Rob, I reviewed some old client feedback to discover clues as to where value arises.

Thanks for a very fruitful session. It was much enjoyed and it helped us considerably in moving forward. Could we arrange a half-day session on Friday 17th?

About half-way through our session I started to get clear. I now know what I want to do. It was like the recent sessions with the team where you were totally skilful, professional and effective.

Last time you facilitated a session with our staff, I felt a huge surge of energy unleashed in the company.

A friend brought me your fax while I was in hospital. It was the best medicine I could have had. Your clarity of thought regarding my situation and my options was like the shining light of reason. I know now with absolute certainty where I want to focus my energy next year. Thanks again Tony.

Participants reported:
- increased confidence to do consulting work
- improved communications with clients
- greater professional impact on clients
- enhanced ability to influence client
- increased ability to plan projects
- improved problem-solving capability.

Managers reported:
- consultants having more influence with clients
- consultants conducting more effective client meetings
- improved quality of consultants' work
- use of consultancy model to plan work.

- 87% of managers felt that participants are actively applying what they learned.
- 77% of participants rate this one of the best courses taken.
- 25% rate this as the best course ever taken.
- 74% managers feel it was worth the cost; rest (26%) say it's too early to judge.
- 100% managers intended to send additional consultants.

You have a capability more than most to talk business language. This can be made use of in one-to-one counselling and various soft skill areas where others have an incapability to tread. You do well in teamwork and facilitation.

The material you developed was rated by customers as excellent, world class. Evaluation ratings are consistently 4.5 on a five-point scale. Some participants spontaneously commented: 'These are the best courses I have ever been on'.

The last two days have been most useful. I am interested in the methods you are using to track projects. You helped me to zoom in quickly on the progress and the issues. I have been having lots of ideas, getting creative again. I would like you to consider doing a course for our people on 'consultancy skills and project management'.

I want you to return to a pure coach/mentor role. Your background in psychology and your closeness to our work here will be a great advantage in addressing certain questions.

You are fast, like a laser, getting to the heart of the issue. You produce work at a pace. We think the same way.

You are highly disciplined and organised.

You are exceptionally well-presented as a consultant.

It was a most productive meeting. You added tremendous value. I am gaining the value of a day's consulting in half a day.

You facilitated us well. You're good at summarising and reflecting back, giving us a clear focus, helping to clarify our thoughts.

You played both a visible and a private facilitation role.

We got on well: I'm technical but you understand the political agenda. You had a very strong influence. You understand human behaviour better than you care to admit. You have an enviable ability to push people gently in the right direction.

Whatever you are charging the company it's not enough!

Our work together was one of my peak life experiences.

Monday 4 September 1995

I shared with Barry an insight about generative conversations. He quickly understood what I was really talking about:

- the potential value is embedded
- your role is extracting the value for the organization
- you are about mobilizing the sleeping giant of the client's resources.

We talked about this book as a personal milestone, a transition, a rite of passage.

Wednesday 6 September 1995

Had a fax from Joe in which he expressed the value that Page Consulting can add to an organization. This value is organization transformation: processes to create vision, achieve mobilization, build learning, coaching to develop the organization and continuous learning.

Value through gaining the client's view
It is always more interesting to hear someone else's view of your work. I still wanted a fuller discussion as what was written on paper was not self-explanatory.

Monday 11 September 1995

Today Tom walked to school on his own. Helen and I stood watching him as he set off. He kept looking back until he turned the corner.

Tuesday 12 September 1995

Lunch today with old client who has moved to a new company. I conducted a conversation on value: it came very quickly to the point of how the business creates value and how he creates value personally.

Value through generative conversation
The discussion with the old client today was following a simple framework for defining and tuning up the value the client brings personally to the corporation – rather like tuning a violin or a carburettor. It felt very relevant but easy, focused and natural.

Monday 25 September 1995

Finally finished the book. Made 10 copies at Kall-Kwik. The next stage is for various people to read and comment. Then a final rewrite before submitting manuscript in December.

Wednesday 27 September 1995

Discussing a project in a local authority, I learned a lot about the context. Here are a few extracts:

It is important to understand what it's like to run something that's regarded as a pile of rubbish. People are dying and getting boarded up in council flats, rubbish is not being collected, people are abused and in abject need. Customers get an appalling double hit: low service and high cost. People inside develop a hard crust, ignoring the abject need, blaming others, not taking responsibility.

Can everyone be brought into contact with the external realities or does it all have to be through the CEO? The end state we are aiming for is adult–adult, removal of the hard crust that separates people. Levels of distrust are very high.

Challenged by tough context

The depth of the local authority problems are clear – deep political and ethnic divisions, deep trauma, confusion, conflict, inability to listen, closedness and negativity. Solution: Prepare myself to be tested to my limits!

Tuesday 4 October 1995

Phoned Fiona, a consultant, whom I have not met, and who had left a message for me. She remembered the 'How to Spot a Faker' article in Management Consultancy in 1992 and said that it expressed what she and her colleagues were feeling at the time. They were planning to leave a large firm and set up on their own. I felt good about this. I felt appreciated. My work was making a difference.

Garth asked me to a meeting with vehicle-leasing company. He said he would value my 'youthful gravitas'. Lunch with Personnel Director who outlined some difficult personality issues in the marketing team. We are being asked to run a teambuilding programme.

PROJECT PLAN

CLIENT: VEHICLE LEASING COMPANY

OCT

1. BRIEFING WITH PERSONNEL DIR.

WHOLE DEPARTMENT TEAMBUILDING PROJECT

We agreed to meet the MD and the Marketing Director and then to consider whether or not it was wise to proceed. It seemed that we could easily fall into a dishonest collusion here where we (the MD, Personnel Director, Garth and myself) are lined up against the Marketing Director; he detects this and so pays lip-service only, while inwardly resisting the teambuilding activity.

Value through careful contracting
This job sounded risky. We were careful to gain control over the situation, making it clear that we might or might not wish to take it on. There is a delicate balancing act at this stage: saying 'yes' and saying 'no' in just the right places.

Sunday 8 October 1995

Helen has been wonderful this week, looking after my Dad. She took him shopping on an electric trike, cut his toenails, washed his hair, wheeled him to Georgia's harvest festival. Today I drove him back to his home on the south coast, near Brighton. The car was loaded with all manner of equipment for the return journey. It was sunny all the way. We unloaded and picked grapes, flowers, tomatoes and apples in the garden.

After lunch we ate ice creams on the beach. The sun was glinting off the sea. It was warm. Dad zimmered slowly over the pebbles and stood overlooking the sea while Georgia and I went to the water's edge and played throwing pebbles in, putting our hands in the water, running up to the sea then running away again to keep our feet dry as the new waves advanced. I felt sad.

Monday 9 October 1995

Enquiry received about using Navigating Change in the National Health Service.

Wednesday 11 October 1995

Worked on proposal for Israel job. It is staff research. The client wants change, not just a piece of research and a report.

As I write this I am struck by the fact that 'staff research' is a flawed paradigm. By contrast, a group constructing their own force field analysis, defining problems and structuring tasks that they can work on themselves has real power. However, there is a real sensitivity – a reluctance amongst management to participate themselves and to give away power plus a fear of anarchy, revolution, mutiny.

Thursday 12 October 1995

PROJECT PLAN

CLIENT: VEHICLE LEASING COMPANY

OCT

1. BRIEFING WITH PERSONNEL DIR.
2. MEETING WITH MD + MARKETING DIR.

WHOLE DEPARTMENT TEAMBUILDING PROJECT

Morning meeting with MD at vehicle-leasing company. He knows there is buried conflict in the marketing team and wants it brought out. Garth and I retained the right either to say no or to amend the arrangements. I think the MD found this irritating; he just wanted speedy resolution.

Then a meeting with John, the Marketing Director. He seemed positive, smiling and open to us, but Garth reminded me that he was unaware of the problems. There are deep personality differences. It is all pretty poisonous stuff. John expressed his willingness to participate in a teambuilding event. He has agreed to us meeting each of his direct reports before the event.

Value through holding firm
In these early meetings we were shifting the definition of

the job to something that was ethical and stood a reasonable chance of success.

Friday 13 October 1995

At a meeting over lunch with a client he said he does not want to go on being a bad client. He felt it was plain from my book draft that he has been unreliable, letting me down, making promises and then not being able to live up to them. I said I have this perfectionist thing but I have to live in the real world: I recognize what it is like working in a big successful company in 1995.

He said that I have reached a certain life stage where my most important needs are satisfied, allowing me to rise to the challenge of writing this book. He needs to get to a similar point in his own life. It is a life-stage thing. He is knuckling down now and not over-committing himself.

Challenged by client withdrawal

I felt let down. This client seemed to be bringing our business relationship to an end, at least for the present. At the same time I noticed he was taking control of his life in a positive way and, whilst I regretted what was happening and feared the loss of income, I felt that, on balance, he was right.

Monday 16 October 1995

Today the job with the vehicle-leasing company was confirmed. The work has been redefined along the lines we proposed: top team one week followed by a full meeting of 50 staff the following week.

Challenged by stretching enquiries

I noticed that the jobs currently available are challenging me more, requiring me to draw more deeply from myself. This applies to the local authority, the recent facilitation course, the vehicle-leasing company and the Israel project. In each case, a standard approach would not deliver a worthwhile result. I rather liked the challenge. Solution: the challenge is always there in every job. Take care to notice it.

Monday 23 October 1995

Network meeting outside Maidstone. I walked into an atmosphere. The other two had read the book draft, and it had raised a whole series of questions. I listened and drew out their concerns as best I could. I suppose the effect was that the book speeded up our getting to know one another. Until this point I had been on a bit of a pedestal and the book presented me warts and all, which I think was rather disappointing!

Challenged by colleagues' misgivings
I was really surprised at how difficult our initial discussion was. I did not know what effect the book would have. I was pleased the effect was discernible and available for discussion. The feedback itself was useful in understanding how to manage expectations surrounding the book and to make reading it a productive experience for the reader. Solution: listen, enquire, summarize, record and embrace others' misgivings.

Wednesday 25 October 1995

I woke up early. Several thoughts are buzzing round my head and I want to capture a couple of them.

Charter of rights and duties during development. A while ago I was discussing conditions needed for deep learning to occur at a local authority. I remembered a 'United Nations Charter of Rights for Children' that I noticed in Kingston Hospital Children's Dept. It says that every child has a right to:

- express themselves and their feelings
- freedom of information
- freedom of choice without coercion.

Very few workplaces live up to these simple principles in the way they deal with adults. We treat people at work as being sub-human. We assume they have surrendered their basic human rights in accepting a contract of employment.

My local authority client remarked that the issue is two-sided: not only does everyone in a workplace have these as rights but, in order for others to claim these as rights, they have a duty to provide them to others.

Next topic. How have conversations with Helen over the years helped to nourish my work?

- first in her sceptical stance: there is nothing new under the sun; BPR is only a conglomeration of recycled old theories
- showing me the real, heart-wrenching difficulty of introducing a quality ethos into Shell
- her precision in methods, measures, key performance indicators
- her auditing skills and factual 'no bullshit' stance
- sharing feelings about consultants hired to do work she can do
- by discussions about female dilemmas in the workplace: hard women make career progress but lose something in the process
- experience of being in a hot team
- challenging me to integrate my work persona with my home persona
- her belief that we can have what we want — setting attainable stretch goals.

This quick brainstormed list also makes me realize how little I might acknowledge others for their contribution. I am so conscious of my own performance that I do not always notice the value that others are contributing.

YOUR RIGHTS	YOUR DUTIES TO OTHERS
To Express Yourself (incl. feelings)	To allow others to Express Themselves (incl. feelings)
To Information	To Provide Information Freely to others
To Freedom of Choice without coercion	To Provide others with coercion-free choices

CHARTER OF BASIC HUMAN RIGHTS (AND DUTIES)

Value through providing a charter

I find that, for a development programme to be meaningful, people have to engage honestly with it, and a simple charter that spells out such rights and duties may be needed. Otherwise we are dealing with covert manipulations and bullshit in all the conversations. Going round in circles gets us nowhere – unless the situation can be made clear and reliable we just create a lot of confusion.

Value through partnership

I have started to think about forming Page & Partners Consulting. If I can acknowledge others' contributions more, I may be ready to work in partnership, building something bigger and stronger, instead of continuing this lonely crusade.

Monday 30 October 1995

Seminar in Birmingham with Allan Pease, the body language expert. He was a short, stocky, well groomed quick-fire comedian, entertainer, salesman.

Value through humour

Allan Pease reminded me of the importance of entertaining an audience – of the physiological effect of telling a joke.

Tuesday 31 October 1995

A colleague told me I was underselling myself. He asked me why Anita Roddick wrote her book. I said to share her thinking and views on business with a wider audience, to win people over to her values and beliefs. And yet I seem to have a fear of self-promotion. He told me I was a highly accomplished consultant, not into client dependency or collusion, really wanting to do something different in consultancy, something valuable. Lots of consultants are hungry for an alternative framework. There is a real business opportunity here.

Challenged by selling myself

This is just a different mode of operation. When I sell, I suppose I have to pump up my ego and I then find it difficult to listen properly. Solution: my colleague suggested I take a clear stance – for example, 'I don't have all the answers – I have warts too – but here are some of the things concerning me'.

Tuesday 7 November 1995

Confusing evening after three days of immersion in teambuilding at the vehicle-leasing company. We did good work. Everything was said, but was it? At the dinner table the Personnel Director joined us. After dinner he took us on one side and told us he was disappointed at the results of the teambuilding programme so far. He had noticed patterns of eye contact and seating preferences and a continuing avoidance of the Marketing Director. He concluded that the conflict was still 'buried'.

PROJECT PLAN — CLIENT: VEHICLE LEASING COMPANY

OCT   NOV

1. BRIEFING WITH PERSONNEL DIR.
2. MEETING WITH MD + MARKETING DIR
3. DESIGN+PLANNING
4. TOP TEAM INTERVIEWS
5. TOP 7 MANAGERS EVENT
6. FULL 50 EVENT
7. TOP 7 EVENT

WHOLE DEPARTMENT TEAMBUILDING PROJECT

Challenged by deeply entrenched behaviour

I was disappointed that the team appeared not to have changed. But we were only half-way through. Solution: recognize that it takes time to bring everything out and achieve a shift.

Friday 10 November 1995

Meeting with the publisher. I provided copies of comments from all 19 readers of the draft. He was positive and excited. I felt his support. We agreed that I would edit and focus the diary entries around the transformation theme and deliver the manuscript by the end of December.

Saturday 11 November 1995

To France for the day. It was Armistice Day and 50 years after the end of the Second World War. In the bustling duty-free area at Folkestone a two-minute silence was announced.

Value through silence
Everyone observed the silence. Two minutes is a long time for children. I felt a real power in this silence: a shared thought, a memory of the horrors of war, a hope that we have learned the lessons, an awareness of Bosnia, Northern Ireland and Africa, a desire never to fall into this horror again.

Sunday 12 November 1995

This year our house is filled with piano music. First Tom, then Helen and Georgia started lessons. Tom is making great strides forward. Georgia is losing interest. Helen is coming on. I love to hear her play 'Lullaby in Birdland', a Chopin prelude in E minor and Rondo Alla Turka by Mozart. I feel this music deeply. It changes my mood, making me melancholic, misty, stirring my energies.

Wilderness session. Very good turn-out. We were clearing a large area ready for National Tree Planting Week: there are 70 trees to be planted. The BTCV (British Trust for Conservation Volunteers) leader turned up on his bike. He said this was a textbook project. I was introduced to him as one of the founders. I told him Isobelle had got us organized with plans, meetings, actions etc. The project is really gaining in momentum.

HOUSE IS FILLED WITH MUSIC

Value through long-term nurturing

We have been involved in this project for nearly five years. We can see slow but steady progress. This has more staying power than anything we could have created overnight, say, by hiring a bulldozer. It is becoming part of people's lives (parents, children and teachers). It is being built into the curriculum and education process.

Monday 13 November 1995

Vehicle-leasing company. Today was special. Garth's voice and credentials (he works with the United Nations) at the outset were very impressive. He energized the group of 50 with his opening address.

We had a fun afternoon in five smaller, cross-departmental groups doing five exercises:

- a blind walk for trust
- charades for communication
- sorting cards for organization
- building a Lego tower for leadership and delegation
- making a collage for creativity.

Each group had a tutor who was a manager untrained in facilitation. Other managers rotated between groups joining in the exercises as 'equals'. Each exercise took 20 minutes followed by a 10-minute review.

By the end of the afternoon groups were performing faster and more effectively. On the Lego exercise the early teams were struggling but the later teams were making profits of

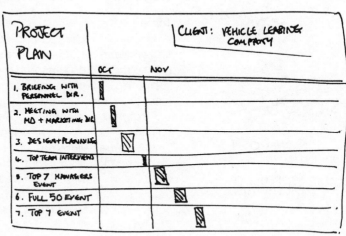

PROJECT PLAN

CLIENT: VEHICLE LEASING COMPANY

	OCT	NOV
1. BRIEFING WITH PERSONNEL DIR.	▨	
2. MEETING WITH MD + MARKETING DIR	▨	
3. DESIGN+PLANNING	▨	
4. TOP TEAM INTERVIEWS	▨	
5. TOP 7 MANAGERS EVENT		▨
6. FULL 50 EVENT		▨
7. TOP 7 EVENT		▨

WHOLE DEPARTMENT TEAMBUILDING PROJECT

£20 million and £35 million. This was important: proof of the improvement to work performance that comes from getting to know and like one another, from process reviews, from giving and receiving feedback, from teambuilding.

By 7.30pm we had a room full of 50 enthusiastic people. You could feel the energy buzzing. Five (non-management) volunteers presented their lessons to the whole group. Their confidence surprised us all, not least their bosses. There was speed, applause, energy, support.

The Personnel Director arrived for a drink at 8pm and immediately noticed the effect – the positive wave of energy.

Value through simple team exercises and reviews

Fast, measurable improvements to performance. If every work group went through this afternoon you could double or treble their performance and put them on a path towards continuous learning. Very exciting!

Tuesday 14 November 1995

Today was also special. We knew we had to rake through some shit in order to sustain the positive energy from the previous day. Garth was able to bring to life a metaphor about compost and roses: you need shit (compost) to grow roses. He did this in his big voice. He filled the room.

First we used fishbowls. We briefed ten managers while the other five groups discussed yesterday's collages. Then the managers sat in a circle of chairs in the centre of the room talking about what they thought the others thought of them while the rest of us sat in the larger outside circle, listening. Each of the five groups had a turn: ten minutes each, guillotine, applause and next group. Then coffee.

After coffee, fearing that some things had still been left unsaid we asked people in pairs to come up with the 'unmentionables': that had still not been expressed. They wrote these on bits of paper and put them in a bin in the centre of the room. We read each item out. Some were really meaty: sexism, racism, favouritism, male managers, overtime pay, I do not feel comfortable with John, Robert, etc.

We speculated that there might still be more 'compost' but, after two processes, it was time to move into Vision and Pathway. We filled the walls with yellow Post-Its. At the end there were high levels of positive energy. The coach arrived at 4pm, and everyone (except the senior managers) departed.

The senior managers shared their reactions:

'Some came with trepidation, others intrigued, open minded but looking forward to it.'
'They all left in a different frame of mind, they were really getting into it.'
'It was amazing. As the five games progressed, you could observe how the groups became more effective from one to the other, The tutors (assistant managers) told us the groups were taking less time and performing more effectively.'
'In the event, no one did try to disrupt it.'
'I noticed self-discipline coming into my own group of staff: someone tried to be destructive and it was the team that dealt with her, I did not have to.'
'We saw characters we have not seen before.'
'I was amazed at the interest of more junior staff.'

Value through large-scale mobilization
In a peculiar way this job was the culmination of what I have been learning for the past two to three years. It was a transformational event – a large-scale mobilization. We proved we can work effectively with large groups. There was a hard and a soft component in it. I provided a clear structure and forward thinking. Garth fitted motivational talks in and around each piece. A third colleague was able to bring out and deal with conflict in the large group. Through balance in the tutor team and by sharing responsibility with the managers, everything was taken care of.

Value through speeding up the digestion process

This was a company run by Theory X despite the known existence and availability of Theory Y, Z and beyond Z. This is not unusual: most companies still use Theory X. Management thought is ahead of management practice by 40 or 50 years.

Our challenge is to close the gap between thinking and doing, to speed up the digestion process, to bring a trusted process for closing the gap. In this case it requires reflection (and personal mastery methods like the diary method or meditation). It also requires 'Trojan Horses' whereby solutions that look like Theory X are sold together with clearly articulated business objectives. Inside the Horse are Theory Y, Z and beyond Z methods which are the means by which the performance objectives are achieved.

Wednesday 15 November 1995

A final day with the senior managers. In the middle of the morning one of them mentioned a habit of backstabbing whoever is out of the room — but usually the Marketing Director. This led to one and a half hours of uncovering and sharing 'unmentionables', including bad breath, the lack of respect etc, etc. After this, the six team members expressed their desire to work together and pledged their support to help the Marketing Director get it right. At lunch we went for a drink. The atmosphere was lighter. The 'cards' were out on the table. Another layer of onion had been unpeeled.

In the afternoon there was action planning, closure and departure.

Value through directness and transparency

Throughout this job the real issues have been avoided. Our job was to help bring them out, to encourage transparency whereby issues are aired before the full team and not privately in whispers. When issues are being discussed we encouraged directness by saying 'I' not 'we', finding specific examples and addressing the person concerned directly.

Thursday 16 November 1995

The phone rang at 7.20am when we were still in bed. Helen answered. Her sister had died.

Thursday 23 November 1995

We came upon a comforting poem by Canon Henry Scott Holland (1847–1918) that, when read out in church at the funeral today, caused us all to sob:

Death is nothing at all . . .

I have only slipped into the next room . . .

I am I and You are You . . . whatever we were to each other, that we are still.

Call me by my old familiar name, speak to me in that easy way which you always used. Put no difference into your tone, wear no forced air of solemnity or sorrow.

Laugh as we always laughed at the little jokes we enjoyed together.

Play, smile, think of me, pray for me.

Let my name be ever the household word that it always was.

Let it be spoken without effect, without the ghost of a shadow on it.

Life means all that it ever meant.

It is the same as it ever was, there is absolutely unbroken continuity.

What is this death but a negligible accident?

Why should I be out of mind because I am out of sight?

I am just waiting for you, for an interval somewhere very near, just around the corner . . .

All is well.

Friday 24 November 1995

Awoke feeling the worse for the brandy after yesterday's funeral. 'Taster' day at Roffey Park re. independent learning sets. Discussion with MD from scientific instrument company reminded me of the hard versus soft dilemma. He wanted to talk about hard, tangible challenges like acquisitions, benchmarking, a distribution centre for Europe, direct marketing. He was not interested in navel-gazing, deep learning or soft processes. He had done enough courses on soft topics while he was climbing up the career ladder.

I have realized that hard results emerge from soft processes. After my exploration of the soft areas of my 'craft', I now want to wrap up my offering in a business envelope – to make the 'efficacy' claim. I want to paint the Trojan Horse nicely, to reach to and deal with the burning issues of business leaders and be relevant to top people. They will not buy process. I need a hard shell on the egg.

Saturday 25 November 1995

In the evening we went to a friend's 40th birthday party. It was in a hall, loud music blasting. We danced to Twist and Shout and some other songs. It was great for us. I felt some real positive energy for the first time since the funeral. Dancing somehow helped to get a lethargy out of our system. I saw some renewed optimism in Helen.

Tuesday 28 November 1995

Meeting with Len and colleague to try to sell the facilitation course. There is still fertile ground but no tangible commitment, no budget and no sponsor. I felt we were clinging on. It was time to let go, face reality and end the project. There was a feeling of sadness.

Len's words were positive and I will remember the project by them:

. . . from our work has crystallized a whole set of meetings management skills, tools and methods.'

Brainstrust session in the evening. The presenter told a story of a hard-headed Texan business man who said to the consultant, 'You've got ten minutes to tell me what value you can add to the business'. How you answer this is my current burning question. You are faced with a choice to talk about hard or soft, results or methods, content or process. If you talk about methods their eyes glaze over, if you talk about results they want to know how. So, as a consultant, you are in a double-bind, a Catch 22; there's no clear solution.

What I learned from discussing this with a (psychoanalytical) colleague was most interesting. You have to talk hard results not soft and fluffy processes. Why? Because of the dynamic going on between you and the Texan. It is called Reaction Formation. The Texan is holding you at a distance and is resisting 'intimacy'.

If you talk methods at this point, you are keeping your distance and playing his game. If you talk results you are putting him into a 'therapist's double-bind': either he joins you in talking about results (which interests him) or, as usually happens, he also becomes interested about how you produce results and asks about your methods. Either way it is a win–win. The best way is to talk about hard results and, when the Texan shifts the conversation to methods, he's interested and the ten-minute time limit no longer matters!

This applies not just to Texans but to all senior managers.

Value through ending a project
It had been dragging on endlessly. No one else seemed willing to bring it to a close. Once we agreed to end it, I had a feeling that the value produced could be realized in other ways, in other projects. Instead of being locked in disappointment, negativity and forlorn hope, we are freed to move on to a new positive, energetic phase.

Value through the therapist's double-bind

We all have buried motivations, resulting in compulsive repetitive behaviour, denials, avoidances and so on that are below consciousness. Often, as consultants, we come up against the client's subconscious considerations which block their access to value from us. We can find ways to drive the client responsibly towards this value. An example of this is a question used to circumvent a CEOs denial: 'Do you want to be right, or do you want to get rich?' The businessman's answer is 'get rich' and, in choosing this, they elect to find out how to get rich from you as their consultant!

Wednesday 13 December 1995

Looking back on 1995, my first thought is that I have suffered many kicks in the face. The business has not moved smoothly ahead. I have been the 'dreamer' rather than the 'pragmatist' in too many situations. But you can't be all things. . . .

Then I realize the progress I've made in various areas of life. I wanted to be bold and courageous in bringing Flow to life and I have. I have engaged in many generative, transforming conversations, with individuals and in groups, where the discussion has been true, real and connected into deep motivation. I have been instrumental in bringing out embedded conflict and in creating the right emotional conditions for some quite difficult work. I know that this creates real change and enduring value. I have also completed a book.

We are appearing on other radar screens now. We had change management enquiries from several large corporates including the civil service, Hackney Borough Council, London Underground, Marriott Hotels, the National Health Service, National Semiconductor, Oracle, Railtrack, Shell, St Ivel, Whitbread and Unilever.

Completing the book turned my energy inwards again for a while but, after distributing the last draft, I felt the support of clients and colleagues. This work is putting my feet on to the ground, making me express what I believe. I feel less of a dichotomy now between home and work. I notice with interest that Georgia has started producing 'Georgia's Real Life Storybook' and Tom has followed with 'Tom's Super Stories'.

As I look forward to next year, there are two major projects lining up – one public- and one private-sector. There is work due to take place with the management consultancy, a hotel company and the market research client. I am booked to give a talk at a Brainstrust meeting. I am getting together with three colleagues to develop an open course for individuals managing change in organizations. I am also starting to promote the diary as a tool for continuous learning in each training course I run.

I want to be active, projecting energy outwards in talks about this book. I want to become really pragmatic in the expression of these ideas. I want to engage in lots of generative, transforming conversations, bringing oxygen to ignite the spark of change!

REFLECTIONS

Reflection on the integrate phase

What was really going on?

The previous phase was idealistic. By contrast this phase was more realistic and pragmatic. New beliefs and practices were lived, challenged and refined. Opportunities were seized for reaching out to impact on others and experimenting (with mixed results). New powerful processes were trialed and proven to deliver results.

In the summer, business seemed to evaporate and everything seemed to stop. Writing the book consumed vast amounts of time and distracted me.

In the autumn, I rediscovered my desire to operate at the most senior levels of business and I became interested in making my offer highly pragmatic and appealing. I became certain that visible hard results are the product of invisible soft processes.

Compared with the start of my journey in January 1993, at the end of this phase I have an extended awareness and a heightened sense of responsibility with a greater interest in family, community and world events. I have a new desire to amplify what I am doing in the world by building in partnership with others.

What is my theory about why?

In the previous phase a strong, initial, ideals-driven enthusiasm was born, which brought with it a blindness to a changing business context. I drove fast and naively into clearly visible obstacles, surprised at the pain on impact!

My offer was not articulated; it was nebulous, lacking in structure, realism or pragmatism. This was confusing for clients. There was no declaration and no easy means for clients to understand and believe in the work. No wonder there were wobbles.

For three or more years a reconstruction of the business has been taking place. At the beginning of this I spoke the hard, results-oriented language of business but the offer felt empty, so I sought enhanced value and authenticity.

I then explored and developed the softer areas of my craft to bring greater power to my work while running a successful business. While immersed in this exploration I gained deeper insight into the underlying human dynamics of business. For a short period in this phase I was unaware of being disconnected from business imperatives. The loss of two large projects acted as a warning signal! In the summer I refocused on how to deliver business value from my work.

At the time of writing this I am ready once more to wrap up my enhanced offer into a business envelope. I feel that it's important to provide the greatest possible impact and value, to work at the most senior levels, to reach far out into the world.

EXERCISE

EXERCISE: CONVERSATION FOR VALUE

Work with a partner to share an experience of a generative conversation.

Start by choosing a specific project as the subject of your conversation.

Behave as a consultant, using the following questions, drawing your partner out, accessing both facts and feelings, finding their energy, summarizing, recording and guiding them gently.

1 Who are the stakeholders in this project and what are their interests?

2 What is your value-creating role?

3 What have you achieved so far and what is missing?

4 **What really matters to *you* about this project?**

5 **What new possibilities for value are there in this project?**

Discuss how you both felt during the conversation, then repeat with your partner acting as consultant to you.

Part III
REFLECTION
ON THE
REFLECTIONS

The value theme

Q: What do a CEO, a nurse, an advertising account director, a works manager, a social worker and a management consultant all have in common?'
A: 'They all create value through their relationship with other people.'

The diary commentaries so far have included over 170 specific ways to create value through other people. You can reference these through the index. Look at any single item and consider what new 'value-creating possibilities' it offers you in working with your clients. But what does this all add up to in a more general sense? What are the most common blockages to value? What are the worst mistakes you can make? Are there any general principles? To answer these questions I'll try to summarize what I learned about value and what to do about it. Will this point to a new way of working with clients? I think so, yes.

Rearranging deckchairs on the *Titanic*

The most common block to value is when a consultant becomes entranced by the 'task' or problem itself and does not attend fully to the 'relationship'. Client criticism of doctors, shop assistants, computer specialists and management consultants is unanimous on this point. It applies to all types of consultant from the 'wire benders' (technical specialists, hands-on doers) to the 'arm wavers' (generalist, hands-off talkers). Our work can become as pointless as rearranging deckchairs on the *Titanic*.

The failing is understandable because, at first glance, the 'relationship' is difficult, irrational and unpleasant. You might prefer not to notice when your client's eyes start glazing over, when you are not being listened to, or suffering misunderstandings, feeling manipulated, experiencing inexplicable bad feelings, feeling afraid, receiving unreasonable demands, being treated like a dishcloth, being typecast, being unable to do your best work, or when the other person is saying 'yes' but not meaning it. You naturally ignore this or blame the client.

In a stable, traditional society you might easily classify situations, predict people's behaviour and gain a sense of control in each relationship. But modern life is a game of musical chairs – a turbulent world where old certainties are breaking down, social and power structures are in meltdown, job roles and corporate structures are in continual flux. New situations are constantly occurring which are unpredictable and difficult to understand. As a result, everyday, you can catch yourself and your clients going through the motions, not fully tuned in to each other, operating on different wavelengths.

The first man and woman

Let's step outside this box for a moment. Imagine the first man and woman. They have no children, no siblings, no living relatives. Let's say they have equal strength, unlimited amounts of time and money, no commitments and they both have something the other one wants. I'll not specify what. This is the simplest human relationship: two free agents, unencumbered by loyalties, by history or culture. It is up to them to communicate their wants and needs and to establish a fair exchange. Both have the freedom to walk away if their needs are not met.

What does 'value' mean to both of them? Simple: getting their wants and needs met. What does 'creating value' mean? Meeting the other person's wants and needs. Easy isn't it? There need be no pretence; burning questions can be articulated and responded to directly. But what is the 'task' for both of them? Just an abstract term – an idea of some actions you have to take to deliver value within the 'relationship'. This definition of task is important.

Business reality

Now let's return to reality. By comparison with the previous example, each human relationship is a confusing mess, like a politician with a mistress: encumbered by power inequalities, implicit assumptions, unvoiced expectations, communication blocks, hidden loyalties to third parties, unfulfilled promises, embarrassments, norms, manipulations, denials, guilt and so on. It is amazing that anyone ever frees themselves sufficiently from this mess to give or gain any value from others at all.

And in each business setting there is an additional element – the powerful, ever-present but invisible hand of the corporation bringing its own requirements and cultural baggage. How do we cope with this reality? As best we can, in a state of mild confusion, stressed out, by suppressing anger, or in a rage, blaming others, hiding our true agendas, with defensive aggression, or by going for a run. In other words, we cope through a variety of personal and idiosyncratic ways. Everyone is overloaded; our fuses are blowing. We're creating turbulent interference patterns, sucking one another into dangerous or confusing whirlpools. With all this going on, no wonder we cling to the task and tune out from our client at times. But by doing this we make ourselves isolated and ineffective: we miss the point – the value-creating purpose – of the task.

The Hiroshima Mindshift

Let's briefly step outside the box again. I'd like to describe the 'Hiroshima Mindshift'. I'll quote first from a widely respected mathematician and social scientist, Kurt Lewin, writing in 1947:

Before the . . . atom bomb, the . . . physical scientist was hardly ready to concede to social phenomena the same degree of 'reality' as to a physical object. Hiroshima and Nagasaki seem to have . . . driven home with dramatic intensity the degree to which social happenings are both the result of, and the conditions for the occurrence of physical happenings.

A 'Hiroshima Mindshift' in consulting means shifting our attitude to embrace the social reality (of the relationship with our client) which gives rise to the physical reality (of the task) which in turn impacts back into the relationship. We each face a choice about whether to stay in a fool's paradise of task-driven confusion or to make the mindshift which reconnects our work properly into a value-creating system.

Two roads

Now let's get really practical. You meet a client to discuss a problem, work request or enquiry. Which question comes first to mind: 'Why' or 'How'? The two questions lead down different roads. If you begin with 'How?', you move straight into task definition; like the client's humble servant you rush down the road of satisfying their probably ill-considered request and, in rushing to action, you surrender the right to question for value. Later, you may be frustrated by 'shifting goalposts' and 'unreasonable' client behaviour.

If you begin with 'Why?' you are led to the 'value target', connecting you with stakeholders' wants and needs. You obtain a fuller and more robust task definition. But if you pursue 'Why?' for too long the client becomes frustrated, wishing to discuss specific solutions. Remember the client may want to shed responsibility for the problem on to you and, by holding 'Why?' and 'How?' questions in balance, you achieve a sharing, collaborative discussion – a form of helping the client without letting them off the hook too easily. This method, which requires an assertive stance, can clean up much of the confusion that exists in the client relationship.

Tuning up your value

Let's continue with a few points about tuning up value in the client relationship.

There is so much advice it is sometimes difficult to know what to do in the real-time pressure of a meeting. A good solution is to forget all the advice and to start by relaxing, enquiring and listening. Begin with 'Why?'. You do not need to talk about 'How' your method works until the client asks. If you find yourself in opposition to the client, avoid getting bogged down in a win–lose debate and try reframing (see exercise: New Synthesis, p. 177).

This is the basis for a style of interaction that is clear, equal, honest, culturally neutral and manipulation-free. You can call this win–win, but most people's win–win falls short of this.

You can tune in directly to the 'value target' using the exercise, Conversation for Value (p. 240). You can also cultivate other methods for tuning in to the client, such as explicit contracting conversations (two-way discussions of wants and needs), time-out process reviews ('Let's stop a minute and look at what's going on here . . .'), noticing the client's energy and learning reviews ('Let's discuss what we have learned so far in this project . . .').

You can review the overall transaction that is occurring with your client and recheck its appropriateness. For example, is it 'We do it *to* you', 'We do it *for* you', 'We do it *with* you', 'You do it *to us*', or what else? Are you a 'willing pair of hands', a 'superior expert', 'an overbearing autocrat' or an 'equal partner'?

Interdependence with others

Some consultants behave like warriors and others as Uriah Heep-like humble servants; these different stances mask different assumptions. Ultimately the creation of value with others is facilitated or blocked by your assumptions about yourself in relationship to others. For example, you might see your success as more important than the other person's. This is the short-term view of desperate people.

In my view, a different assumption creates greater and more enduring value: namely, your success is interdependent with the other person's; it is impossible ultimately for one person to succeed at the expense of the other; it must either be win–win or we both lose. If you follow this path, your wants and needs have to be expressed directly and matched in an explicit exchange with the client, just like the first man and woman in the example earlier. This style is assertive, fair and equal.

Recognizing interdependence with others is an important key to value that applies in every role and relationship from CEOs to Olympic coaches to IT consultants.

The whole business as a value-creating system

During my journey I started to think more about the business as a whole. Take the example of a healthcare company seen as a value-creating system. Before we attempt to

create value here, we need to recognize what value means. The principal 'stakeholders' are, say, customers, employees, suppliers and shareholders. For each of them value means something different:

- The customer perhaps wants economically priced drugs that work.
- The employees and suppliers want fair payment, security, growth opportunities and so on.
- The shareholders want profit, rising share prices and dividend payments.

This is the 'value context' for our task. By recognizing this and understanding it our work can connect with the value goals of many others. If we ignore it we are forced to make wild guesses and wrong assumptions based on a narrow definition of a task or problem.

Every business is a value-creating system. The challenge for consultants is to make an intervention that enhances value within the total system. By contrast, consultants often talk about 'creating change' as a worthy pursuit, taking a very narrow focus, seeing one set of stakeholder's needs (for example, shareholders) as being more legitimate than those of others (for example, customers or employees).

Relationship is hard, task is soft

I used to think that relationship was soft-headed and easy, and that, by contrast, business value was about something hard-headed that we had to fight blindly for. I now realize that it is the other way round: to be task-driven is a soft-headed, naive and incomplete view that only ever succeeds in the short term by waking people up. A focus on relationship is not soft: it requires tough, assertive honesty and provides the fertile conditions from which emerge the peak levels of creativity and performance that everyone in business is seeking.

By seizing the opportunities highlighted here to unblock value and make it flow, we can all combine our strength together. Superior business performance arises from individuals in effective two-way relationships creating superior value. One plus one repeated across a corporation and across society can equal three . . . billion! Your challenge is to find the two-way value in each relationship and to get the value flowing.

The transformation theme

I asked William Gates III if some people were allergic to computers – in which case his whole take on the future might run up against human fallibility.

He looked at the carpet pondering. 'There are only people who psyche themselves out of it because in adult life they are not used to being confused,' he says seriously. 'When you're a kid and you're learning it's okay because a lot of things are confusing and you persevere with it.' (Extract from interview, *Sunday Times* 12 November 1995)

I have presented a five-phase personal transformation covering a three-year period. What have I learned about transformation from this? In this chapter I'll cover what I think transformation means, why it is relevant to you and to your corporation, how it is achieved and what risks and rewards to expect.

What is transformation?

The dictionary defines 'transformation' as, 'a change or alteration especially a radical one'. The word is used in mathematics, linguistics and physics as well as in human change. It implies something fundamental, at the core. Marilyn Ferguson, in *The Aquarian Conspiracy*, distinguishes four basic ways that we change our minds:

- 'change by exception' where we accept anomalies as the exception that proves the rule: 'I'm right except for X'
- 'incremental change' which occurs bit-by-bit, leaving the individual unaware of having changed: 'I was almost right, but now I'm right'
- 'pendulum change' where one closed system is replaced by another: a promiscuous person becomes a prude, a religious enthusiast becomes an atheist: 'I was wrong but now I'm right'
- 'paradigm change' where the brain harmonizes conflicting ideas into a powerful new synthesis: 'I was partially right before and now I'm a bit more partially right'.

The first three ways fall short of transformation. The fourth way – paradigm change – is transformation.

To simplify, we can think of transformation as a three-stage route:

1	Thesis	what I first believed to be true (for example, 'Swans are white')
2	Antithesis	new contradictory information (for example, 'Some swans are black')
3	Synthesis	new belief based on harmonizing thesis and antithesis (for example, 'Most swans are white, but some are black')

Why is transformation relevant to you?

See if you can relate to this. In my childhood in the 1950s and early 1960s we had a clear routine to life. We had family meals three times a day, roast on Sunday, cold meat on Monday, shepherd's pie on Tuesday. . . . We went to church. I joined the cubs and the choir. I played the cello. The monotony of life was broken by occasional camping holidays or trips to the coast, festivities at Christmas and birthdays. Sounds idyllic doesn't it?

I accept this picture of stability might be somewhat distorted by a child's eyes and an adult's distant memory but, in the space of 40 years, people's lives have undoubtedly changed beyond all recognition. Factories, coalmines and whole industries have been closed. Home cuisine has become international. There is a vast choice of goods in every supermarket. We wear new colourful clothes. Children have computers. Households have TV, videos, satellite links and CD players. Technology has stepped forward. Public services have been privatized and internationalized. Markets have opened up. Goods are sourced from across the world, and jobs are no longer for life.

When I left school I knew a lot about competitive struggle, about suppressing and denying emotion in the quest for success. I knew nothing about continual adaptation or learning, except in the sense of accumulating increasingly up-to-date knowledge. I knew very little about other belief systems, or how beliefs get formed, or emotions and how to deal with them. How about you?

We now live in an era of unprecedented turbulence which constantly triggers our inner emotions. Yet our awareness of inner change is very low. Stress, mid-life crises, divorce, violence, crime, drug abuse . . . it is easy to list the signs of problems in people's lives. In the US the huge cost of stress-related illness is starting to be quantified. In the UK doctors and hospitals are beginning to realize just how much of their workload is due to stress and psychological factors.

Countries are pouring funds into education for children to enable their workforces to compete in world markets. Life is a race to pass exams, to get a job, to get a pay rise, a promotion, to win success. In the Western world, the old religions are in decline. Business has become a new religion, but a void of meaning remains which the old Eastern religions have been starting to fill.

It is as if all this was unexpected. We have been naive, applying first aid to people through the health service after their predictable life crises instead of teaching them to anticipate and adjust in advance. We deliver unbalanced news coverage and seek to inculcate out-of-date and incoherent beliefs. We foster unrealistic expectations that lead to negative debilitating emotions such as guilt, embarrassment and anger. We nurture the critic inside us. We let people lose themselves under the dead weight of all this. We leave them dragging the heavy millstones of dissonance. We give no lifelines – no learning about how to digest life experience, how to deal with emotion, how to reframe and transform problems. Tragically, people are both afraid of, and are being denied, the liberating benefits of transformation.

'Mid-life crises' and the 'male menopause' used to be embarrassing aberrations that triggered transformation and rebalancing after years of keeping the lid on a pressurized pan. Like nervous breakdowns, these experiences were negative and not to be referred to in polite conversation. But in reality life is filled with stresses and traumas such as redundancy, divorce, serious illness, death, childbirth and working parenthood.

We need to discover for ourselves, then develop and teach a new competence, empowering individuals to 'digest' their own life experience, regularly readjusting and recovering quality of life in the face of external turbulence. Instead of denying and hiding our frequent, traumatic inner experiences, we can start to feel good about our new-found ability to reframe, adapt, evolve and learn. This is why transformation is relevant to you.

Why is transformation relevant to our corporations?

You have been involved, as a stakeholder, with countless corporations perhaps as a customer, employee, supplier and/or investor. Corporations have provided you with opportunities throughout your life. What's wrong with them? Plenty! In the face of your changing requirements as a 'stakeholder' they are extraordinarily unresponsive to change. Look at schools, look at government, look at IBM, look at the banks, look anywhere. They all share this problem. Reg Revans, who spent most of his working life encouraging business people to engage in real, effective learning, said that, for a company to survive, it must be learning and adapting (L) faster than the changes (C) occurring in its external environment: L must be greater than C.

Hamel and Prahalad, in *Competing for the Future*, agree:

. . . few companies that began the 1980s as industry leaders ended the decade with their leadership intact and undiminished. IBM, Philips, Dayton-Hudson, TWA, Texas Instruments, Xerox, Boeing, Daimler-Benz, Salomon Brothers, Citicorp, Bank of America, Sears, Digital Equipment Corp, Westinghouse, Dupont, Pan Am and many others saw their success eroded by the tides of . . . change.

As a stakeholder you put your faith into companies, supporting them with your energies and your purchases, but if L is less than C you can be certain of a shock coming. According to Hamel and Prahalad, many companies are giving the illusion of success through 'denominator management' – that is, by cutting costs rather than nurturing new revenue opportunities to sustain the business into the future. Much of our current turbulence could be the hangover from past denominator management.

A recent survey of 160 US and European businesses (reported in the *Financial Times*) found their greatest success had been in a few centrally-driven change endeavours such as organization design, strategy and downsizing. By contrast, these firms were struggling with initiatives that require behavioural change. Rounds of cost-cutting had left employees feeling insecure and demoralized. Difficulties in changing people's behaviour were expected to become more, not less, acute once companies start focusing on growth and innovation rather than cutting costs. Only when externally imposed threats to survival are present has it been possible to galvanize a workforce.

But why should it be necessary to build up a deficit, to allow L<C until there is a threat to survival? Could it be because companies comprise people? Companies not changing are the consequence of people not changing: a dinosaur strain is clinging on to its past instead of learning and adapting to create a positive future. Could it be anything to do with people dragging their millstones of dissonance, unable to digest their life experience? *'We have enough problems of our own thank you very much. We are keeping the lid on life'*.

In the early 1980s I remember the top 50 managers in the company I worked for attending a Crosby programme to inculcate the language, culture and practices of quality management. This was the first of many corporate change programmes I am aware of in which huge investment, inflated ambitions and promises were followed, inevitably, by compromise, disappointment, cynicism and resistance. And yet incredibly organizational change has become a huge growth industry for consultants, business educators and publishers. Oscar Wilde once said that second marriages are the triumph of hope over experience. To me this looks more like a lack of corporate awareness, a denial, a blind, compulsive repetition, not learning important lessons that explain failure and enable future success.

It seems that corporations, despite putting great effort and investment into change, do not know how to conduct conversations with people (customers, employees, suppliers and investors) that would really engage them and bring about transformations. If we could develop a new competence – to engage people in transforming conversations – could this be the key to breaking the Matsushita curse?

How is transformation achieved?

The beginning of personal transformation is absurdly easy. We have only to pay attention to the flow of attention itself. Immediately we have added a new perspective. Mind can then observe its many moods, its body tensions, the flux of attention, its choices and impasses, hurting and wishing, tasting and touching. (Marilyn Ferguson, *The Aquarian Conspiracy*)

At the personal level of transformation, the above quote says it all. Simple methods are needed to support you in paying attention to the flow of attention. One such method is the diary method. Other people prefer meditation, personal coaching, counselling or therapy, or group dialogue meetings.

Continually throughout daily life there are small tensions, feelings, stirrings of energy which we barely notice because they are not immediately relevant to the task we are engaged in. These small tensions often signal a gap between what we are doing and what we believe more deeply. When become truly aware of these tensions, you start to recognize patterns and this recognition draws more attention in, so that you start to speculate and discover reasons. Over time, attention does its work. The practice develops a momentum of its own as can be seen from the diary extracts earlier.

Instead of simply living within your 'thesis' (as I did at the start of the diary), you begin to notice contradictory evidence which leads you to explore further (as I did during 1994) and the 'antithesis' builds strength. Then you have created a tension which the mind works actively, but invisibly and unconsciously, to resolve. In my case this resulted in insights or 'flashes of the blindingly obvious' occurring towards the end of 1994. This was the birth of a new belief system – a 'synthesis' of thesis and antithesis. The next stage, which took place during 1995, was to live, test and integrate the new beliefs .

In a corporation it would be ridiculous to require or reward people for keeping diaries or meditating, but there is plenty that can be done. A series of opportunities can be provided that help to awaken people to transformative methods and reduce their fear of them – workshops, external courses, personal coaching, dialogue meetings, talks about personal transformation, visits from specialists in many diverse fields.

Breaking through corporate conformity

The real barrier to corporate transformation is the pressure to conform. We are all naturally reluctant to make 'career-limiting' statements. It generally pays not to upset the boss. Hofstede, who did pioneering work on national cultures, speaks of culture as 'collective mental programming'. Corporate cultures that are highly tuned into performance become stifling, leaving no space for transformation. The 'official line' on most topics is obvious, and disagreement is not only discouraged but punished by isolation and dismissal. It becomes all 'thesis' and no 'antithesis'; therefore no 'synthesis'. You only ever have a very limited kind of conversation.

Hamel and Prahalad, in *Competing for the Future*, speak of the need for genetic diversity:

> . . . we know from the biological sciences that the long term health of any population of organisms is dependent on a minimum level of genetic variety. The same is true for . . . a company . . . one has been able to observe a startling lack of genetic variety across whole industries.

Goss, Pascale and Athos, in *The Reinvention Roller Coaster*, highlight an obscure law of cybernetics called 'requisite variety': 'any system must encourage and incorporate variety internally if it is to cope with variety externally'.

Variety means disagreeing, bringing out, rather than suppressing, conflict, using diversity as a strength, noticing and working through differences.

Making space for transformative conversations

During these three years, on a number of occasions, I became involved in conversations that I felt to be special. They had a generative quality, producing new ideas and insights. They had a compelling quality: both participants became gripped or immersed in them. Both participants' thoughts and ideas seemed to weave together producing a new, never previously stated, view of reality that was owned by both parties. There seemed to be 'synthesis' taking place, in real time, from the interplay of 'thesis' and 'antithesis'. Each of these conversations has been highly memorable. They seem to me to contain one of the keys to corporate transformation. If you could replicate the conditions that give rise to these types of conversation, then you would have a means with which to break through conformity, to harness variety and produce the new synthesis that represents transformation.

So what are the necessary conditions? The central quality of these conversations is a 'flow state' in which both parties are opening their minds, sharing their deeper insights with the other, listening for meaning and building bridges that connect both views into a new synthesis. It is similar to the flow state described for an individual skilled worker by Mihayal Csikzentiminhalyi and referred to by James Martin in *Enterprise Engineering*:

> Flow is a condition in which a skilled worker is using a learned capacity with intense concentration . . . a designer manipulating ideas, a tennis player on a court, a copywriter perfecting an advertisement, a planner, a person in deep thought. The condition of flow is euphoric if the person is using their skill well. The person is barely aware of the passage of time . . . he needs long periods without interruption . . . he curses every telephone call. You cannot instantly switch into this state. It takes

time to descend into the thought process, perhaps ten, perhaps 20 minutes of concentration before the ideas start to flow . . . The brain manipulates a complex web of ideas, slowly organising them and creating structures. Whenever he is interrupted, the links among the ideas are lost; the ideas might vaporise; it takes time to re-establish the threads. . . . Concentration is so intense there is no attention left to think about anything irrelevant.

My flow state differs from the above in that it takes place between two people. Peter Senge and David Bohm have described the conditions for 'dialogue' in a larger group. These are similar: setting time aside, listening, accepting, building on ideas, connecting.

In the reality of the workplace, how might you make space for, and gain value from, such special conversations? You are trying to open up a 'space for transformation', separate from the 'cut and thrust' of today's performance-driven work. You can start by experimenting with some one-to-one 'Conversation for Value' (see exercise p. 240). Set aside, say, two hours, with just two people, in a quiet room.

Who should be involved initially? Hamel and Prahalad, in *Competing for the Future*, give examples from Kodak, Sony, Sharp and Canon where new value is created in the 'white space' between current operating units:

. . . future opportunities are unlikely to correspond perfectly to today's business definitions. . . . 'white spaces' refer to opportunities that reside between or around existing product-based business definitions.

So choose two people from different parts of the business.

What should they talk about? Give them a hard, business agenda that would appeal to the CEO, such as product development, acquisition, finding new distribution channels – something that stretches their thinking beyond the current, performance-driven frame.

After experimenting with these conversations, they can be developed in at least two dimensions: first, interpersonally, by building in two-way feedback that accesses deeper differences between the parties; second, pragmatically, by translating the emergent thinking into specific projects that can be resourced and executed to realize the new value.

Transforming an entire corporation

How do you engage everyone in an entire company towards transformation? With difficulty is the answer, but there are certain conditions that are important and often seem to be missed.

Gandhi's work in South Africa and, later, India provides a powerful example of mobilizing large numbers of people. He said numbers were less important than quality and truth. Marilyn Ferguson describes this approach in *The Aquarian Conspiracy*:

[it] . . . derives its power from two apparently opposite forces: fierce autonomy and total compassion. It says in effect: I will not coerce you. Neither will I be coerced by you. If you behave unjustly I will not oppose you by violence but by the force of truth – the integrity of my beliefs. My integrity is evident in my willingness to suffer, to endanger myself, even to die if necessary. But I will not cooperate with injustice. . . . Together we can solve the problem. It is our opponent not each other.

She also quotes a stirring passage by Eknath Easawaran from his memoir *Gandhi the Man*:

Finally after weeks of deliberation the answer came to Gandhi in a dream. . . . The government had imposed a law . . . making them [the Indians] dependent on a British monopoly for what is, in a tropical country, a necessity of life [salt]. . . . it was the perfect symbol of colonial exploitation. He proposed to march with seventy-eight of his most trusted followers to the little coastal town of Dandi, some two hundred and forty miles away, where salt lay free for the taking on the sand. When he gave the signal, everyone in India was to act as if the salt laws had never been enacted at all.

By the time he reached Dandi the non-violent army had swelled to several thousand. . . . Then at the moment of dawn, they went quietly down to the water and Gandhi, with thousand of eyes watching every gesture, stooped down and picked up a pinch of salt from the sand.

The response was immediate. All along India's coastline huge crowds of men, women, and children swept down to the sea to gather salt.

How is anyone able to trigger such a huge release of human energy? The key seems to be in a style of leadership, described by James McGregor Burns, where the leader senses and transforms the needs of his followers:

I don't see followers simply as persons holding a collection of static opinions. I see them as having levels of needs. . . . The effective leader mobilises new, 'higher' needs in his followers.

The truly great or creative leaders do something more – they induce new, more activist tendencies in their followers. They arouse in them hopes and aspirations and expectations. . . . (*Psychology Today*, October 1978)

How different is this from the oppressive threats and elaborate manipulations at the heart of many corporate change programmes! We seem rarely to give time and permission to people to express their truths. Rarely do we embrace all the truths of all the stakeholders (employees, customers, suppliers, investors). We allow a privileged few to define the truth in a narrow sense. We then thrust this narrow, sanitized, corporate version of the truth at people in a way that is reminiscent of a totalitarian state. Diluting and diminishing the power of our programmes in this way will destroy our collective future.

The transforming conversation described earlier is a way of reaching deeper-level needs and arousing higher level hopes, aspirations and expectations. After experiments with this method, the leader might begin to engage larger groups, whilst protecting the critical conditions needed for the deeper and higher truths to be expressed. Ultimately we might reach a position where we can gather all the stakeholders into the same room.

Together, we can discover and share the many truths. We can give time and permission for truths to emerge. We can allow contradictory views to co-exist instead of rushing to consensus. We can uncover 'what is' and allow this potent compost to produce, in time, a new synthesis – a qualitative shift, a transformation.

This is a delicate process, well described by Ralph Stacey (1993), requiring tolerance of ambiguity and confusion – rather like living on the edge between order and chaos. The glittering prize for this uncertainty is a self-organizing system which serves the interests of all the stakeholders without requiring heavy-handed management intervention at any point. Such an organization can be more efficient, more effective, more energetic and more enduring.

What are the risks and rewards?

The challenge to you, and to every company, is to develop the new competencies of transformation summarized here.

Your risk is that transformation takes on its own momentum. You can never fully know in advance what forces you are unleashing. Initially there may be some turbulence and difficulty such as I experienced in my argument with Edward in January 1993. This could have destroyed my business, my income and my self-esteem.

You must guard against the risk of breaking trust with the people closest to you. Once broken, trust can be irrecoverable. How do you manage this risk? Start your transforming conversations here and keep yourself open and tuned into what matters to the person(s) nearest to you. Make sure you stay strong at the centre of your life in this way. Start here and work outwards.

Why bother with transformation at all? Because, unless you face reality, you are storing up trouble for yourself later. Would you rather keep the lid on life, be like a steaming pressure cooker – volatile, unpredictable, rarely in equilibrium with yourself and the people around you? You know that, if you constantly seek reality and truth, ultimately you can achieve a more harmonious and enduring equilibrium.

To put it in a nutshell, transformation is the only known path to enduring quality, personal satisfaction and peak performance.

The learning theme

Inner voice 1 (anxious child): 'I feel blocked. I don't know what to say. I sense that the next bit is important. We're getting to the heart of the method. I'm concerned this might not seem as if it is anything to do with business'.

Inner voice 2 (mature adult): 'Let's put that on one side for the moment and get on with describing the method that you know works.'

The Real Life Learning method

For some people the desire for continuous learning has been satisfied – mistakenly I believe – by attending increasing numbers of courses and conferences. This may be necessary but it is not sufficient to generate the kind of learning that produces full adaptation to a changing world and, beyond adaptation, the discovery of creative new possibilities for enhanced performance.

This book is an example of a new learning method which I use in my consulting work supporting various challenging corporate change and development initiatives. I call the method 'Real Life Learning' because instead of learning from theory, it is about learning from real life.

Just as food enables a child to grow to their full adult height, your digestion of experience in a changing world enables you to achieve what really matters to you in life. The method described below helps to reveal your habits and behaviour patterns and free you from them. It shows how you can be nourished and made strong by your life experience.

The method can be used personally – as I did, in my diary – or by a coach, facilitator or consultant to assist their client's learning.

Inner voice 1 (anxious child): 'It's time to delve into it now. I'm getting warmed up here.'

Inner voice 2 (mature adult): 'OK, take it slowly. See if you can keep the reader with you. Set out the case for continuous learning.'

The case for continuous learning

Why is change so difficult? You begin to find the answer when you look at people's behaviour. You see patterns repeating – for example, passivity, anger, obsession, avoidance, blame. These patterns are habits, routines, programmes, ways of coping with daily problems. Like an autopilot, they fly the plane, without calling on the pilot's attention. This is fine provided that destinations, the beacons and routes are fixed. But if the context is changing, running on autopilot can be life-threatening: only old known signals are discerned and responded to; new signals pass unnoticed unless you return to manual control. It becomes plain that today's habits and programmes are deeply rooted and dangerous obstacles to change.

Now look at yourself. How much do you know about the habits and programmes that are running you, locking you into a repeating and possibly life-threatening present? Most of us would answer that we know little of these. They are largely invisible. They hide themselves from us. We are afforded occasional glimpses from other people, but feedback can feel strange and we may not know how to make use of it. We may feel more comfortable ignoring it.

Life is a rich meal, not always easy to digest. If we listen to ourselves we can often hear rumblings and the occasional pains of digestion. But under the pressure to perform in a busy life, we have become used to ignoring the emotional ups and downs. In business we often say, 'What counts is behaviour and performance', 'Let's be real, concentrate on what we can see, get on with the job in hand'. This blind approach is incompatible with a desire for continuous learning.

The emotional undercurrent to life that we become accustomed to dismissing as mere 'noise' in fact contains the early warning signals – the triggers for change and learning that, if attended to, will offer the needed new directions.

Inner voice 1 (anxious child): 'We need to show when it's just noise and when to blow the whistle and call time out.'

Inner voice 2 (mature adult): 'That's a bit like deciding whether or not a client is resisting. It's all about deciding when to make an intervention.'

Deciding when to intervene on life

In his book, *Flawless Consulting*, Peter Block highlighted a simple and effective method for handling client resistance. He presented a three-step method that requires us to listen to ourselves, notice when our hackles are rising and notice how the client is behaving. This monitoring activity provides the early warning signals of resistance. Once we notice resistance, we stop the conversation and confront the client gently with something neutral and non-judgemental that describes what we have noticed. Then we fall silent and wait for the client to respond.

The resistance-handling method contains some of the clues to continuous learning. There is an advanced sensitivity – a tuning in to one's own and the other person's feelings, a detachment from the hurly-burly of conversation, a desire to find out what is really going on behind the behaviour, a recognition that continuing with the conversation after a certain point is pointless; you need to get behind it.

So how do you get behind what is actually happening to what is driving it? The answer is that you must make an 'intervention' that temporarily halts the stream of events. It can take place any time but at certain times it is both more important and more productive. Here are three important triggers for interventions:

1 **DO–DO–DO cycles**: when you notice that your own behaviour has become repetitive, has fallen into a pattern. Much management behaviour seems to be like this. Your environment is constantly changing, so if your behaviour is not, then you are falling behind and isolating yourself. This is a clue that you have become fixed or detached and that a learning opportunity is there for you.
2 **TALK–TALK–TALK cycles**: when you find yourself saying the same thing over and over again. This is a sign that you are caught up in some kind of emotional loop. For example, I was talking to a nanny who was recently sacked. Her conversation went in circles, stuck in the past events, in her preoccupations with the family she used to work for.
3 **EMOTIONAL HIGHS AND LOWS**: when you notice either that you are very happy or very low-spirited. This is a sign that some background events, below consciousness, are affecting your emotional balance. A low might arise from a combination of unfinished activities, a doubt about something you are doing in your work or your life, or a contradiction between your deeply-held values and the way you are behaving. A high might arise from the reduction of tension when a job is completed, a result that you had long hoped for actually arriving, or a stressful current tension being removed.

How do you intervene?

Now that you have some triggers for intervention, the next question is *how* do you intervene on life? There are a couple of questions that I find useful here:

Learning Question 1: 'What's going on right now?'

Learning Question 2: 'How do you feel about it?'

I use these questions to initiate my daily diary entry. It is surprising what comes out. These questions stimulate you to express what is lurking just below consciousness. The same questions can be used when coaching, facilitating or consulting with clients.

Inner voice 1 (anxious child): 'What we've said so far only scratches the surface. We have to describe how to get behind the events and the feelings to what is producing and driving them.'

Inner voice 2 (mature adult): 'Yes, you've got to expose the underlying rules, implicit assumptions and values, the "theory in use", which is like the computer's operating system. You're getting into some deep waters here.'

Delving beneath the surface

We all know how deeply ingrained habits can be. Addictions are a good example of this. A 47-year-old man recently had his second heart attack, was warned by doctors that his alcohol and cigarette consumption was endangering his life, but still finds it impossible to give either up. Many of us, too, know about the difficulties attached to being overweight.

The first two learning questions do not seem to help in many of these cases. For example, when I asked the nanny referred to above those questions, they just circled continuously in her TALK–TALK–TALK loop.

The solution in this case was to use the Peter Block approach and to gently confront the pattern with 'You seem to be going round and round. I'm wondering what would be needed to break you out of this endless cycle.' These words force a break; they stop the repetitive flow so that you can probe deeper towards an explanation. When I am writing the diary, I achieve this by using two further questions:

Learning question 3: 'What's *really* going on?'

Learning question 4: 'What's my theory about it? (= why?)'

Again, these two questions can be used in one-to-one client–consultant conversations to trigger deeper learning.

The theory first expressed in response to Learning Question 4 may not be 'right' but it will reveal 'implicit assumptions', making them accessible to learning and change. We are always, in every situation, working to some kind of theory but, until we know what it is, we are its victims not its masters. Once you know your theory, you can judge for yourself whether it works or not.

As a consultant, once the client reveals their theory it is possible to add value by highlighting contradictions between their behaviour and their espoused theory. With the diary method, you look for these contradictions yourself.

Although this is not enough to break a habit or pattern, becoming explicit about reality and the theory underlying it serves to create dissonance which in turn builds up the energy and will to change. It does have an important loosening effect, making further change easier to achieve.

Inner voice 1 (anxious child): 'I feel disappointed that we cannot go further with breaking habits in this method.'

Inner voice 2 (mature adult): 'Yes. Remember the alcoholic though. Be realistic. Some things require deep, lifelong therapy. Some habits are not susceptible to change. Why not say a bit more about finding the energy and the will to make change?'

Finding the energy for change

When you feel stuck, your energy is low and, like a carthorse wearing blinkers, your vision is also restricted. From this position it is difficult to learn. You can raise your energy in preparation for learning by reflecting on past achievements and by listing current incompletions. Once you have done this, your energy tends to be higher and you are ready to do some concentrated work on the current dilemmas by identifying what really matters to you about it.

This leads to the next three learning questions I use in writing my personal learning diary:

Learning question 5: 'What have I achieved to date that I am proud of?'

Learning question 6: 'What is incomplete or missing?'

Learning question 7: 'What really matters to me?'

The last question reminds me of the control I want to have over my life, helps connect me to my values and brings out intentions that I want to see realized. These give the solution to any dilemma in outline form.

Inner voice 1 (anxious child): 'There's still a piece missing. There's lots of navel-gazing here, but we have not shown how to get to real practical solutions.'

Inner voice 2 (mature adult): 'So far you've focused on reality, the theory in use that drives reality, the energy or will needed for learning or change, but you do not know where you are going. You still need to find some positive direction to move in.'

Finding a positive direction

It is dangerous to define your direction without considering other people and groups who also have an interest in the outcomes – for example, your boss/client, your customers, the shareholders and your staff. Equally, you need to consider your own best interests and the value you seek to create in your own life. Once you have explored these elements, then it is time to formulate specific action. Here are the relevant questions:

Learning question 8: 'What value do you want to create for other stakeholders?'

Learning question 9: 'What value do you want to create for yourself?'

Learning question 10: 'What do you propose to do next?'

All the time, as with coaching, there is a balance to be struck between reality (talking about what is really going on), energy (maintaining the climate and the will to change) and direction (what to move towards). The expression of your personal theory underpins all three of these and empowers you to take control of change.

Inner voice 1 (anxious child): 'I'm worried that this is getting theoretical. Will the reader be interested enough to try it?'

Inner voice 2 (mature adult): 'You'd better describe clearly how to get the diary started. But, remember, this book provides a compelling example of the method in action.'

How do you get started with the diary?

What should you write in a personal learning diary? This part is easy: you can write whatever you want, whenever you want! I hope the ten questions above will help you.

Remember, the method takes you way beyond a business view to a whole-life perspective: personal, professional and corporate. It goes beyond objective or intellectual analysis, capturing also your subjective moods and feelings.

It is best to do it regularly. It is best to write about what is of greatest interest at the time of writing: either the positive events (energizing you) or the negative (blocking you). It is useful to review your entries occasionally to obtain deeper insights.

This book gives you an example of the range and diversity of entries in a personal learning diary.

Inner voice 1 (anxious child): 'The personal component is so important. I feel we have rather glossed over it here.'

Inner voice 2 (mature adult): 'Yes, if it is just an occupational or professional log, then the writer will never access the deeper energies which will drive their change. It is from exploring the dissonance between personal values and business life that much of the deeper learning is available. But don't worry. The ten learning questions are designed to draw in the personal component. We can only go so far in explaining this. The proof is in the pudding. Let the reader discover this.'

Finally let me remind you of the benefits. The Real Life Learning Method described here is a way of liberating you from the patterns and behaviour that trap you in a repeating present, providing you with a helicopter view on your own life. Try it and monitor the benefits you get. In my experience, this simple method has brought a priceless enhancement to life.

Towards ever-improving performance

Inner voice 1 (anxious child): 'It's time to close but I still have a few things to say. Most business books are all about performance. CEOs, and everyone else for that matter, want their companies to perform. Performance helps you survive when the climate is tough. We haven't spoken enough about performance.'

Inner voice 2 (mature adult): 'That's because you've used a different word: value. By searching for value you have been tuning up performance. You have shown through transformation how everyone can reach a new level of performance with less desperation and greater ease. Perhaps you had better make this explicit.'

First, some performance metaphors. A car can keep on driving with its handbrake on and still reach 30, 40 or 50 mph. Initially there will be heat and sparks and the fuel consumption will be low. After this, the wheels may be damaged and the braking ability will be destroyed, but you would hardly notice until you encounter an obstacle in the road!

Plants in fertile ground will usually flourish and produce more fruit and seed than those in stony ground, which might die. For each plant there are optimal conditions of soil, climate, nutrients that produce peak performance.

Mismanaging the human dimension

Like complex machines and plants, people perform best under certain optimum conditions, but there are some key differences. Unlike machines, people are resilient and highly adaptive: we can go on living even under hostile conditions of huge oppression and deprivation, such as in prisoner-of-war camps and under ruthless dictatorships. This resilience brings both an advantage and a disadvantage. In some cases – for some people more than others – the will to survive and perform is strengthened under hostile conditions. However, on average, across all people and situations, hostile conditions ultimately cause people to give up, to die, to close themselves to opportunity, to suffer stress and to burn themselves out. In the extended coping period before giving up, the individual adopts exaggerated and desperate behaviour patterns which show their worst neurotic side, become blind and deaf to external stimuli and maintain a highly oppressive stance with others.

To believe that such conditions enable peak corporate performance or transformation is to misunderstand human nature and the lessons of history. This approach treats people as expendable.

By contrast, companies which protect and shelter people from external realities, shield staff from the requirements of other stakeholders, require people to leave their intelligence in the locker room and create passive dependency are under-performing and fostering complacency through oppressive overnurturing.

The high-performance position lies between desperation and complacency. This position has the same characteristics for companies as for individuals. It is a position where people are value-seeking not security-obsessed, are seeing not denying reality, where conflict is seen as a fuel for transformation not as the opportunity for a war. Every ounce of intelligence is being used towards a common purpose. Listening, looking and seeing 'what is', and transforming contradictions into a new view of reality – just like the search for value in this book – fuels the continuous adaptation process.

Inner voice 1 (anxious child): 'OK. But how do you know if you have the balance right between desperation and complacency as a person or as a company?'

Inner voice 2 (mature adult): 'We need to show how you get hard results from soft processes and how monitoring energy is a key to maintaining balance and sustaining peak performance.'

Energy as a key performance measure

If you were planning to run a marathon what preparations would you need to make? Perhaps you would get fit, become single-minded, choose your pace and practice, then, over time, build up your strength. How would you know if you were succeeding or not? You could measure speed and distance but if you fall short, what do these hard measures tell you about how to build sustainable performance? Very little. They are hard and objective but also detached and after the event. They tell you where the gap is but not how to close it.

If also, not instead, you monitor your energy during the practice, then you gain the keys to performance improvement. You can ask whether you were low on energy at any point. You can ask how you felt at the end of the practice – ready to repeat, or ready to rest, or totally demoralized and lacking in any inner reserves? The answers provide real leverage for improving performance. You can increase your food intake, adjust your pace, build up your strength for, say, the uphill phases . . . choosing specific solutions that build energy where it is needed. Higher performance emerges from beneath the surface of the hard results, by looking inside at the softer process, at the 'energy'.

Re-energizing yourself

Let's look at an energy-efficient approach to performance. In managing your energy towards peak performance you may, early on, become aware of a simple cycle of human energy. When you score a goal you gain a boost, replenish your energy and become stronger to score more goals. By contrast, when you set out to do something but do not finish it, then you suffer a continuing energy loss until either you complete or let go of the intention. In a busy life where you are making promises all the time, the de-energizing effect of incompletions is cumulative, like applying the brakes while you are still pressing on the accelerator: you experience more friction and consume more fuel.

The first stage in re-energizing yourself is to let go of promises you will never fulfil. Instantly you will begin to feel lighter and stronger. Then deliver on a few overdue promises in the short term and experience the energizing effect of completion. Finally, take more care when making intentions, and when promising and saying 'yes' or 'no'.

The second stage is to tackle more profound matters: values and the smothering, papiermaché layers of unchallenged obligations, requirements and assumptions derived from parents, schools, churches and corporate edicts. By finding these 'shoulds', then sorting, discarding, accepting or and adapting them, you transform layers of stress-inducing confusion into a clear and reliable guidance system for performance that distinguishes you as a powerful, authentic, direct, 'what you see is what you get', probably compassionate, ethical and trustworthy being. This stage offers liberation – a release from stress, dissonance and non-specific anxiety. It releases vast amounts of energy that were previously locked up inside you in unresolved conflict.

I recognize the earliest origins of my journey to 'authenticity' in the unresolved conflict between my parents' humanistic values and the commercial values I adopted to 'get on in life'. Until it was directly tackled, this conflict was stressful and de-energizing. Once the new synthesis was made, I felt tremendous new energy.

This book supports you in re-energizing yourself by providing a logical method, by demonstrating how it can be done, how it is available to everyone and does not require superhuman abilities. The most important prerequisite is a willingness to see and monitor the truth.

What we have said so far about re-energizing you as an individual is equally true of the corporation. I believe that, by applying the same energy principles to the corporation, we can unlock ourselves from the Matsushita curse (p. 5) and gain access to a series of performance quantum leaps. Unless we provide the space for the re-energizing transformation, we lose the race and Matsushita is proved right, but worse, we use up the human capital and kill the goose that lays the golden egg.

Inner voice 1 (anxious child): 'That's enough about the principles of performance and energy. What next?'

Inner voice 2 (mature adult): 'Let's bring it back to our reader who is interested in "value through others" and reach the close.'

How all value is created

All this might sound theoretical, in contrast perhaps to '50 ways to close a sale' and other simple 'how to' approaches. Does it really create tangible value? Yes. How important is this? How much value is generated? The value is huge. We can only see glimpses. A few of the workplace improvement teams (small groups given space to take their blinkers off, look at reality, develop new ways of working) in the healthcare company clocked up value worth $213 million. The computer support consultant who was stuck, succeeded in realigning his energies and made a client presentation which won him new business worth £53,000. The 50 motor vehicle-leasing staff involved in simple team learning exercises improved their performance by hundreds of percent in about three hours.

The real monetary value of this approach is in billions. We have been looking at how to create value through others and of course *all* value is created through other people. So we have been looking at how *all* value is created. This is the sum of all the gross national products of all the countries in the world! I get excited about this but, realistically, I know we have only explored a part of a picture. There is no end to the antithesis out there just waiting to combine with the thesis of this book, to produce a more powerful, new synthesis, and so to advance civilization.

Where are they now?

This book is a product of a three-year interaction between my emerging 'thesis' and the 'antitheses' that others have offered. Although it has often not been easy for me, I have enjoyed, appreciated and gained huge value from the stimulus and challenge from others along the way. Where are they now?

Joe has been busy in Europe helping general managers and their top teams in each country to lead their businesses through turbulent change. He has been bringing change management know-how into the business from ODR, Gemini Consulting, Richard Pascale, Knowledge Based Development and others. He is the most knowledgeable person I have worked with, towering over most of his colleagues in the field of change management.

Richard is now a vice-president. I often forget he is a logistics expert: he is an inspiration to many of us, championing change management approaches that embrace and include people, operating at the frontiers of human knowledge and, at the same time, sticking with and producing tangible benefits from the massive worldwide re-engineering project he is leading.

With Peter, and Richard's team, we produced an accessible new product called 'Navigating Change' that underpins the change management work there. Peter has recently used the product on his travels in Australia, Ireland and elsewhere. Navigating Change may soon be available for use more widely both inside and outside the company.

Len has become a happy and accomplished facilitator of senior management teams. Together with a couple of other colleagues, Len and I developed a prototype and experimental course called 'Workplace Facilitation Skills' from which has crystallized a whole set of meetings management skills, tools and methods.

The healthcare company share price rose 50% this year.

The hotels sector is in upheaval. One client's company has recently taken over another client's company, leaving one of my clients out of a job and considering a new career in consultancy.

The management consultancy firm is adjusting, after some initial staff turnover, to its place in a larger worldwide organization.

Kinsley Lord has merged with Towers Perrin.

The market research company has taken on several new staff and is expanding.

Barry became president of the Institute of Management Consultants in 1996.

What to do next?

If you've read this far, perhaps you are expecting a final nugget – a quick and easy solution to 'life, the universe and everything'. Sorry to disappoint you, but I'll offer what I can, to point the way ahead.

Everyone's life comprises many lessons and a few transformations. This book has described many lessons, but just one transformation in one person's life, and, in describing it, I hope I have made the transformation process plainer, more commonplace, more acceptable and less of a difficulty for some other people.

I hope you might feel challenged to adapt, own and use something of what you have found here. The value lessons might bring you direct economic benefits. You may find you are already embarked on a journey such as mine, about which perhaps you have little choice and which you know will not be speedy or easily accomplished. If so, I would like to hear about your experiences directly. Then perhaps we can start to build a wider network that offers mutual support.

For others in your organization who could benefit from considering the ideas presented here, you can give them the book as a first step. I would also like to offer some further support through talks, development workshops, 'transformative' conversations and dialogue sessions. I need not repeat the tangible benefits accruing from this.

In a still wider sense, I am keen to raise awareness and develop our collective 'transformational space'. I intend to continue writing and working myself in this field, but I am interested in collaborating with others to achieve more.

This rather brings us full circle. I remain Tony Page. I am a management consultant. I am 40. You can contact me at: phone: +44 (0)181 943 1690, fax +44 (0)181 977 1159, email: tonypage@dircon.co.uk.

Inner voice 1 (anxious child): 'Phew!'

Inner voice 2 (mature adult): 'Phew!'

References

C. Argyris and D. Schon (1974), *Theory in Practice*, San Francisco: Jossey Bass.

Peter Block (1981), *Flawless Consulting – a guide to getting your expertise used*, San Diego: Pfeiffer & Co.

David Bohm (1994), *Wholeness and The Implicate Order*, London: Ark Paperbacks.

Mihaly Csikszentminhalyi (1992), *Flow: the Psychology of Happiness*, London: Rider.

Eknath Easawaran, *Gandhi The Man*, Petaluma, Calif.: Nilgiri Press. (Quoted in Marilyn Ferguson (1980). No date given.)

Marilyn Ferguson (1980), *The Aquarian Conspiracy – personal and social transformation in our time*, New York: Tarcher Lutnam.

Robert Fulghum (1986), *Everthing I Ever Needed to Know I Learned in the Kindergarten*, London: Villard Books, Random House.

Tracey Goss, Richard Pascale and Anthony Athos (1993), 'The Reinvention Roller Coaster – risking the present for a powerful future', *Harvard Busines Review*.

Barry Green with Timothy Gallwey (1986), *The Inner Game of Music*, London: Pan Books Ltd.

Gary Hamel and C. K. Prahalad (1994), *Competing for the Future*, Boston: Harvard Business School Press

Michael Hammer and James Champy (1993), *Reengineering the Corporation – a manifesto for business revolution*, London: Nicholas Brealey.

John Heider (1985), *The Tao of Leadership*, Aldershot: Wildwood House.

G. Hofstede (1980), 'Motivation, Leadership and Organisation: Do American Theories Apply Abroad?', *Organizational Dynamics*.

Vanessa Holder (1995), 'Children of the Revolution', *Financial Times*, 12 September.

Kurt Lewin (1963), *Field Theory in Social Science*, Social Science Paperbacks.

Jeannie Marshall (1994), *Energetic Meetings*, Santa Monica: Jemel Publishing House.

James Martin (1994), *Enterprise Engineering*, Lancs: Sarant Institute.

James McGregor Burns (1978), Quoted by Marilyn Ferguson from interview, *Psychology Today*, October.

Michael McMaster (1994), *The Intelligence Advantage – organising for complexity*, Douglas, IOM: Knowledge Based Development.

Tony Page and Ron Hyams (1992), 'How To Spot A Faker – the genuine article will triumph in the end', *Management Consultancy Magazine*.

James Redfield (1994), *The Celestine Prophecy*, London: Bantam Books.

Reg Revans (1982), *The Origins and Growth of Action Learning*, London: Chartwell-Bratt, Bromley and Lund.

Judy Rosener (1990), 'Ways Women Lead', *Harvard Business Review*, November/December.

Peter M. Senge (1990), *The Fifth Discipline – the art and practice of the learning organisation*, London: Century Business.

Ralph Stacey (1993), 'Strategy as Order Emerging From Chaos', *Long Range Planning*.

Lesley White (1995), 'Net Prophet', – interview with Bill Gates, *Sunday Times, News International*.

Index